# Reflections on Eldership

*Insights from Practising Elders*

*Compiled by*
## Laurence Wareing

SAINT ANDREW PRESS
Edinburgh

First published in 2014 by
SAINT ANDREW PRESS
121 George Street
Edinburgh EH2 4YN

Copyright © Laurence Wareing 2014

ISBN 978-0-86153-821-8

British Library Cataloguing in Publication Data

A catalogue record for this book is available from the British
Library.

It is the publisher's policy to only use papers that are natural
and recyclable and that have been manufactured from timber
grown in renewable, properly managed forests. All of the
manufacturing processes of the papers are expected to conform
to the environmental regulations of the country of origin.

Typeset by Regent Typesetting

Printed and bound in the United Kingdom by
CPI Group (UK) Ltd, Croydon, CR0 4YY

# Contents

*Preface*                                                        v

*Introduction*                                                   xi

*Eldership in the Church of Scotland*                            xv

 1  The Road to Eldership                                         1
 2  Promises, Promises ...                                       19
 3  Seeking Spiritual Growth                                     30
 4  Experiencing Change                                          41
 5  Hopes and Dreams                                             52
 6  The Elder as Pastor                                          63
 7  Making Some Things New                                       79
 8  Making Space for Young People                                92
 9  'To See Oursels as Others See Us'                           104
10  Decision Makers                                             114

*Appendix 1: Resources*                                         133
*Appendix 2: Questionnaire*                                     136

# Preface

This study of Elders breaks new ground. The Church of Scotland has already issued handbooks for Elders, discussion guides and courses for the training of Elders. But never before has there been a published survey of what Elders, themselves, are thinking about their function and their responsibilities. This book reveals the seriousness with which today's Elders approach their historic role.

The Scottish Reformation, embodied in the Scottish parliament of 1560, introduced the 'Presbyterian' form of Church government in which lay people, 'Elders', play an essential part. The Episcopalian pattern retained a hierarchy, in which authority was exercised by bishops with little lay involvement. For the next two centuries there was contention between the Presbyterian and the Episcopalian models of Church order. First one dominated, then the other. In 1690 Presbyterianism was re-established as the pattern for the National Church, and it has remained so ever since.

At the Reformation, as a reaction against the hierarchical structure of the Roman Catholic Church, and the power vested in Cardinal and priest, the Presbyterian system introduced lay people into positions of authority.

The title of these lay leaders was taken from the early church. St Paul speaks of 'Elders' as having authority in leadership in congregations.

In *The First Book of Discipline*, composed in Edinburgh in 1560, there is a stated place for 'Elders' – 'seniors' – to be elected by congregations. The seniors, the Elders, were accorded the power to exercise discipline on the congregation. In this way, the powers which formerly, in their entirety, were vested in the Roman Catholic priest, were now being divided. The priest had held the authority to preach and interpret the Word of God, and to carry out spiritual functions through sacraments and prayer. He also had the power to exercise discipline on the people in his care.

The Reformation, however, introduced a two-fold pattern of authority. On the one hand there were 'teaching Elders', and on the other there were 'ruling Elders'. The Minister, as 'teaching Elder', was confirmed as the leader of worship and the preacher of the Word of God and the person who presided at the Sacraments of Baptism and the Lord's Supper. However, the responsibility for exercising discipline, and the power to do so, was given to 'ruling Elders', usually referred to simply as 'Elders'. This not only had the intended effect of limiting the power of the ordained minister, but the introduction of 'ruling Elders' brought lay people into a place of real significance in the structure of the church.

After the Reformation, and after the restoration of Presbyterianism in 1690, each congregation of the Church of Scotland was overseen by Elders who, with their minister, formed what was known as 'The Kirk Session'. The

Elders, having charge of the disciplining of local people, exercised considerable local influence. They could impose public humiliation on transgressors, including punishment such as sentencing individuals to be detained for days in the stocks. By the time of the poet Robert Burns (1759–1796) some Elders in Ayrshire had earned a reputation for both authoritarian behaviour and moral hypocrisy, as exemplified in Burns's poem 'Holy Willie's Prayer'.

As the Scottish legal system developed, and the law-courts became the forum for public discipline, the role of Elders changed and they concentrated on other aspects of the life of congregations. This same focus remains today. While the minister leads the worship and is responsible for Christian education, the Kirk Session is often in charge of all the business of the congregation: caring for the finances, ensuring that the buildings are maintained in good repair, supervising the activities of the organisations.

In 2002, I visited the Federal Republic of Nigeria. As Moderator of the General Assembly, I was representing the Church of Scotland. I met with President Olesegun Obasanjo. He said, 'Nigeria owes Scotland an un-repayable debt. Not only did you bring us the priceless gift of the Gospel, but you brought a tradition of universal education, and you Presbyterians brought the practice of involving lay people, as well as ordained, in the running of the church – preparing us for participatory democracy.' With these words, the President opened for me a new perspective on the significance of the Presbyterian system

In addition to their institutional duties, for more than a century and up to the present time, one of the chief functions of the Elder is to have a pastoral relationship with a number of members of the congregation. It can be seen that this is a development, a transformation, of the Elder's original role as an agent of discipline. Many Elders are assigned a district in which a number of members of the congregation are resident. It is the Elder's responsibility to visit each church member in their home, and to care for their spiritual well-being.

These are major challenges for men and women of any age-group. The book contains many moving accounts of how individual men and women came to accept an invitation to become an Elder, and to shoulder a measure of responsibility for the well-being of the church. Many of those who were interviewed for this book have, admirably, been willing to speak of the anxieties that beset them when they accepted Eldership. But in their quiet reflections they reveal themselves to be people of great integrity, who feel responsible for the good name of Christianity and of the Church. They speak of striving to express a spiritual dimension of life in their relationship with individuals and with the church. One Elder speaks of change:

... Our society has changed in the last 50 years, and is generally more selfish and more cynical and, as an organisation we have to compromise. However we need to remember that, despite these changes, the most important thing is the individual relationship with, and faith in, God and fellow human beings.

I find that I do sometimes have to distinguish between my relationship with God and my relationship with my church.

In a theme which recurs throughout the book, Elders sense that, by their way of living, they are to demonstrate that Christian belief is something worth having. And many of the Elders interviewed speak of being ready to speak of spiritual matters, and of recognising the importance of praying with the church members in their district. But among many such quiet testimonies, one story stands out.

This particular Elder had tried to persuade one young man that he should explore what faith could do for him. But then the Elder left his wife, and his home, and was divorced. Years later he met the young man again, who by then was himself involved in a church. 'I wondered if I had said or done something to help him to that new stance,' said the Elder. 'It was profoundly shocking to me when he went on to say, "It was when you got divorced"'. Up till then, the young man had seen this Elder as essentially better than him, and so he believed that God was really for people like the Elder, and so not for him. But seeing this fallen Elder still believing, the young man thought maybe God could, after all, be for him too.

The book reveals that today's Elders recognise that the number of ordained Ministers is declining. They recognise that a greater weight of responsibility for the running of the church is being devolved on to Elders. Elders can now be found conducting funeral services, preaching and conducting Sunday services in church. One Elder organised a whole district's local churches through his role as Presbytery Clerk. Elders see these new duties as a development of the historic role of Elder to meet the current circumstances.

As the Church in Scotland enters a new age and an era

of uncertainty, this book will provide both stimulus and reassurance. In the pages of this book the Church's 'silent army' of Elders is revealed as remarkably focused on the central place of individual faith, and on the importance of a lively and relevant Church. The book will make helpful and stimulating reading for every Elder. Each Elder will find some comments which exactly reflect their own experience. They will also meet insights which illuminate new areas of their thinking. As a means for Kirk Sessions to examine their strategies and practice the book will be of unparalleled value. The book is a treasure-house of wise reflection.

Laurence Wareing has made available the reflections of this cross-section of Elders. The Church of Scotland in particular, but other churches too, will be greatly in his debt.

John Miller

# Introduction

By and large, elders tend not to talk at length about their role. They will discuss matters at hand – the business of the kirk session, perhaps, or the life of the congregation in general – but talking about themselves is a different matter. Perhaps it is Presbyterian reserve at work, or maybe becoming an elder just feels like another way of engaging with church life; its demands are simply 'what you do'. Or is it simply that they are so rarely asked about it?

Yet might it not be helpful, for a short while, to step back and ask elders the question: Why did you accept the invitation to become an elder and what does it mean to you to carry on in this role? Might it be helpful to them, as well as to others (including potential elders), to articulate their understanding of the role and to compare and contrast their experiences of it? Elders have much to tell each other: about how they share similar concerns and face similar challenges; about how they've grown and developed along the way; about new ways of doing things, of 'being Church'. Such a conversation may raise as many questions as it answers. But it will deliver a sense that no elder and no kirk session is alone in the work they do and the vision they are trying to make real.

This book tries to facilitate such a conversation in an informal way. In the following chapters, each one devoted to a broad theme or question, elders speak to elders. As much as possible, they speak for themselves. Occasionally – by juxtaposing certain viewpoints – they engage with each other, even though they've never met and probably live hundreds of miles apart. Their names and brief explanations are included where it has seemed helpful to place a particular point of view in context. Otherwise names are not included beside every contribution – in part to allow contributors to speak as freely as they wished but also to allow the words to flow with as little interruption as possible. A motif of three stars separates contributions from each different elder, whether named or not.

Over thirty elders have contributed to the discussion that follows. They speak from places as far apart as Shetland and Ayrshire, East Lothian and the Isle of Lewis. They speak from wealthy congregations and from urban priority areas. They speak from the cities and from the hugely varied rural and island settings that make up so much of the Scottish landscape. Some are in their eighties, with many years' experience under their belts; some (though predictably fewer) are in their twenties. Many elders speak with energy, ideas and hopefulness in spades. Between them, like the 35–40,000 other Church of Scotland elders from whom they are drawn, their experience runs the gamut of church and community life. They know their communities, they are involved in decision making, they are aware of what is (or isn't) being done to engage with young people, they worry about church buildings, they are excited when the Church responds to the needs of those with whom they live and work.

The picture is not always rosy – sometimes quite the opposite – but there is a constant commitment to service, especially in the local setting, that unites these particular members of the eldership, the Church of Scotland's so-called 'silent army'.

Together they offer a resource for extending our reflections on the life of the eldership into our own churches, kirk sessions, small groups and private thoughts. Elders and others reading these often quite personal contributions will say, 'I recognise that' or 'I really don't agree with that' or 'That reminds me of …' – and so the conversation will be extended. To help support the use of this book as a way of encouraging discussion, the questionnaire used as a starting point for the book is included as Appendix 2. Also of considerable value to anyone interested in understanding eldership are the responses to the eldership consultation being undertaken by the Church of Scotland's Mission and Discipleship Council at the time of writing and which can be found at www.resourcingmission.org.uk/resources/eldership-consultation.

Thanks are due to all those elders who took time to complete a questionnaire, talk on the phone or meet over a cup of coffee, sharing their stories and experiences openly and honestly. Many thanks also to Ron Clarke and his colleagues in the Church of Scotland Mission and Discipleship Council, and to Roy Pinkerton, who responded with his customary care and wide knowledge to first drafts of the introductory comments and materials.

# Eldership in the Church of Scotland

Elders within the Church of Scotland are ordained for life by a minister and then admitted to membership of the kirk session of a parish. Traditionally they have been tasked with carrying out pastoral and local church-government duties under the guidance of the minster (the 'teaching elder') to whom they give day-to-day support. The kirk session itself is one of the 'courts', or structural building blocks, of the Church of Scotland. The other two are Presbytery (overseeing groups of kirk sessions in a defined geographical area) and the annual General Assembly.

## Serving in a long tradition

The term 'elder' is used throughout the Bible to indicate those who carry out the duties of local government, overseeing justice and, at times, pastoral care. In the New Testament, elders were either important Jewish leaders or leaders in the shared ministry of the early Church. However, exactly how the term is being used within the Acts of the Apostles and the letters to the early Christian communities is not always clear. The term may sometimes simply indicate older members of the community. Rather nicely, C. K. Barrett suggests that when Luke, the writer of Acts, used the word, he had in mind the apostle Paul taking leave of local communities and asking his earliest and most trusted converts to 'please keep an eye on things for me till I can return'.[1]

Keeping an eye on things is what church elders have done in one way or another ever since, sometimes to a degree that would conflict with modern-day expectations of privacy!

The term is not exclusive to Presbyterianism. There are elders in many denominations, though the requirements of the role differ. (Some contributors to this book have experience of the eldership in other traditions, in particular the United Reformed Church and the Society of Friends, or Quakers.)

## Elders in the Church of Scotland

Once admitted to a kirk session, an elder takes on the role of a charity trustee of his or her local congregation. (Occasionally a concern has surfaced in contributors' comments about the implications of trusteeship. Does this mean that an elder's own savings or property are at risk should the finances of their church fall into difficulties? The Church of Scotland Law Department has

---

1 C. K. Barrett, *Church, Ministry and Sacraments in The New Testament*, Carlisle: Paternoster Press, 1985, reprinted 1993, p. 52.

produced helpful guidance in this regard.)[2] As trustees, elders are required to maintain an active interest in the affairs of the session. Where age or other circumstance makes this more difficult, some sessions have introduced the idea of *emeritus* or 'inactive' elders who retain their status as elders but are no longer members of the kirk session. They may of course remain 'useful' to the life of the congregation in other capacities – perhaps by undertaking pastoral visits and other similar duties.

If an elder moves from the parish in which they were ordained, he or she is still an elder of the Church of Scotland but is not a *serving* elder. Normally, once their membership has been transferred to a new parish, they will be invited to serve in their new congregation and to join the kirk session. However, as in the case of two contributors here, it is always possible for an elder to choose not to serve in their new congregation.

---

2 From 'Elders, liabilities and OSCR' – a circular produced by the Church of Scotland Law Department and available in full on the Church of Scotland website: 'So far as is known, no congregation has ever found itself in the unhappy position of being unable to meet its debts to third party creditors and the question as to whether individual office bearers might be required to meet such debts from their own resources has never arisen. It is to be anticipated that with the wish to protect "unlucky" office bearers and protect the good name of the Church, the wider Church may "rally" round and meet any liabilities incurred – except of course in cases where fraud or other criminal activity on the part of office bearers was established and perhaps also where there had been persistent and wilful failure to follow directions from Presbytery in regard to the incurring of the liability ... The General Assembly however requires all congregations to have in place public and employers liability insurance in the form of the standard policies of the Church of Scotland Insurance Company. In addition, a special breach of duty policy has been written to cover special risks and is also compulsory.'

Traditionally, a parish will be divided into districts (usually geographically) and 'district elders' are appointed to visit church members resident in their district on a regular basis. They sometimes speak about 'visiting my "elder district"'.

As well as being a member of the kirk session, an elder may be appointed to attend the higher 'courts' of the Church – Presbytery and the annual General Assembly. Presbytery elders are often appointed on a fixed-term basis. One elder from each kirk session is commissioned to attend the General Assembly every four years or so; elders in a large kirk session may therefore only have the opportunity of attending once in a lifetime, if at all.

## Other roles

Depending on the way a congregation is run (see below), an elder may take on a number of different and complementary roles. He or she may train to chair the session in the absence of the minister. Within the context of worship, though individuals may participate in many ways, elders as a body are at their most visible when assisting with the distribution of the elements of Holy Communion.

A number of elders speak of having also trained to be a 'reader' – a role whose duties are principally, though not exclusively, concerned with the ministry of the Word and the conduct of public worship.

The 'session clerk' (who may or may not be an elder) is the secretary to a kirk session and has a leadership role within it second only to the minister. When a congregation is without a minister (during a 'vacancy' period), the congregation and session is guided by an interim moderator, appointed by the presbytery.

Presbytery clerks have considerable administrative responsibilities for the presbytery and the kirk sessions it represents.

## Different constitutions – different demands

In the stories and accounts that follow, it becomes clear that elders have varying experiences of what is expected of them and how they are able to contribute to congregational life. One reason for this is the variation in the constitutions under which different parish churches operate.

At the time of the Reformation in 1560, the new protestant Church adopted the centuries-old parish system and developed the idea that a kirk session is responsible for all things – both the spiritual life of the parish and its day-to-day 'temporal' needs, such as education, discipline within the community and social welfare. Elders meeting as members of the kirk session determined all aspects of a congregation's life, including property, buildings and finance, as well as the spiritual matters of worship and pastoral oversight. It is from this understanding of the session's functions that all other constitutions have flowed.

A number of variant constitutions arose over time, following the union of the United Free Church and Church of Scotland in 1929. For that reason some elders have experienced a kirk session-plus-congregational board arrangement (in which the congregational board oversees temporal matters) or a kirk session and smaller board of managers.

Under a 'unitary constitution', a relatively new form of church government, a kirk session often relies on smaller groups to look after various aspects of the congregation's life and witness. Members of these groups include, but are not exclusively made up of, elders. The observations of some elders in the following chapters suggest that this is a structure that can give a congregation considerable room for manoeuvre as it adapts to changing congregational and community needs, though it also has an impact on how elders perceive their role within the workings of the church and parish.

# I

# The Road to Eldership

*How do women and men become elders? Are they guided to a sense of call after being encouraged to think and respond to the idea? Do they hear a persistent voice in the manner of the boy Samuel who was called early in life to a life of leadership and prophecy (as told in 1 Sam. 3)? Sometimes a divine signal is indeed very clear, however hard it may be to describe in words. More often, however, elders speak of coming to the role in ways that seem to reveal little of divine activity: because it 'feels right'; because they were caught in the street in a weak moment; maybe because they were the next name on an ever-diminishing list of options; or simply because they 'fell into' the role almost without thinking – it was another step in a lifetime of commitment to the Church. Not that this makes their role and contribution within their local congregations and communities in any way invalid. Far from it. And from their different experiences, many elders offer simple and clear advice for anyone who has been asked to consider taking on this lifetime commitment to an ordained role within the Church.*

On a visit to Jerusalem, *says Donald MacKinnon from Oban*, we walked the road to Calvary and when the tour guide pointed out the station of the cross where Simon of Cyrene was press-ganged into carrying Christ's cross (Mark 15.21–22) I felt very moved and vowed to do more to serve my Lord.

The best advice I was given, by the then session clerk, was 'be yourself'.

\* \* \*

*Maureen Mackinnon, one of five elders in the small village of Portnahaven on the Isle of Islay, was also out walking when she found herself directed on to the road to the eldership.*

I was made an elder in November 2000. I was accosted in the street by an interim minister. It was a hard time for me. My mother had died after having two bad strokes. I had looked after her for three and a half years, which was draining. I wasn't well myself and I was trying to run a business. I was very low. How did I feel? It's difficult to say because I'm indigenous. Your roots go back – you're just part of the village so you do things. I've never thought of it as a burden or a gift. If you say 'yes', you make a commitment. When you signed the formula, you made a vow.

\* \* \*

Although born in Shetland, I grew up within the Presbyterian Church community of Australia after my father accepted a call to the parish of Kirklands, Tasmania in 1950, *recalls Alastair Christie-Johnston*.

I was part of a young, vibrant congregation in the 1960s numbering about 150 communicants (St Matthew's Presbyterian Church, Glenorchy in Tasmania). Three session vacancies were to be filled and I was asked if I'd accept nomination. I was 28 years old at the time, employed as a Field Officer with the Scout Association and an enthusiastic Sunday School teacher. As a son of the manse my life to date had always revolved around the church and involvement was second nature to me. I would not say I experienced a call from God as such – at least not in the way I understand that term. It was more a case of being carried along by the tide. St Matthew's had a dynamic young minister who was a good friend and something of a role model. In retrospect I'm sure he had a lot to do with helping me in reaching my decision. These were exciting times for the Church in which enthusiastic moves were afoot that subsequently brought about the formation of The Uniting Church of Australia.

I felt myself privileged to be nominated to the role and when I was elected I entered upon the work with youthful enthusiasm. I was given a list of communicants for whom I was responsible and was expected to visit them at least four times a year, reporting directly to the minister on any relevant issues that were raised. Most of the elders were of a similar age to me and we took our responsibilities very seriously. Prior to becoming an elder I didn't particularly think about those responsibilities. Willingness to do one's best seemed to be all that mattered.

\* \* \*

*In 1966 the General Assembly of the Church of Scotland
agreed to ordain women as elders on the same terms and
conditions as men. Some years later Sheilah Steven recalls
questioning whether it was right for her, as a woman, to
become an elder.*

Bearing in mind that this was over 30 years ago, my
main question was a theological one. Was the eldership
a role for a woman, given Biblical evidence? Having discussed it with my husband, who is not an elder although
he has been asked several times, he was happy for me to
proceed. I studied the relevant Biblical passages. In prayer
I received the assurance that this was a role that I could
fulfil with God's grace. Interestingly it was not until some
five years later, when I was able to help a member of my
district in a spiritual way, that I 'felt' that God had indeed
called me to the role. Up to that point I felt I was merely
fulfilling a practical role for the church, albeit one that
gave me a sense of fulfilment.

The advice I would give: ask what it practically involves;
attend a training course if possible; discuss it with someone who knows you well; pray for guidance; expect
guidance to be given!

\* \* \*

One woman I spoke to said she felt she was 'not good
enough to be an elder'.

None of us is 'good enough', in the Christian sense. I
was very surprised when *I* was asked to become an elder.
I didn't think I was clever enough or good enough. Also

there were not many women elders at that time. Quite a few people were against women in the eldership.

I think the contribution women have made has been seen to be very valuable. I know the minister at that time was very pleased with the contribution of women and wanted more. Yes, I think he *was* bucking the trend and I believe within the local area there is still one congregation without a woman in the eldership.

More women are being made elders but I wouldn't like to see a preponderance of women over men. I'd want to see a balance. Though there *are* more women coming to church than men, and many of us are widows.

\* \* \*

I cannot say I experienced God's call when reaching my decision, *says Sylvia Davie*. However, it felt right and I felt I had something to offer. At that point I was where I wanted to be in my life. I was content and felt it was time to give God something back in return for guiding me to where I was.

\* \* \*

I had been involved in church life, *says Mima Bell from Glasgow*, in the Girls' Brigade and so on. But when I was asked to be an elder my first thought was, 'Am I good enough?' I prayed and thought at length and, as I did so, I felt as though I had so much more to give to God's service. My minister helped me to understand that God did not expect me to be a readymade perfect elder; that it was only through being willing to pray and learn that I could be an elder.

The only advice I would give another person is to think, and remember that being an elder is not being another committee person; it is much more important.

\* \* \*

I got asked. That's basically it. My personal feeling was that I was never going to put myself forward for it. It was not a great surprise to folk – I'd been to the General Assembly as a Youth Representative. I'd been to a session meeting and I'd been a member of the congregational board. I knew the workings of the church, but thought I'd have to be asked. My experience of elders had been that I found a few of them a bit 'Look at me!' – as if the eldership was a sort of status thing. I didn't want that accusation to be attached to me. The eldership is about serving and humility – that's a huge part of it. So the best way would be to be able to say, 'You asked me'.

Both my parents are elders in the church. My dad's advice was, 'Don't do it'! Why? Because the closer you get to the centre of things, the more of the politics you uncover and the more rigid it can be. And it gets more stressful. That was also my experience *before* becoming an elder!

\* \* \*

*Just prior to being ordained as an elder, William (Willie) Scobie recorded his feelings on the matter in a letter to his minister, Revd Ian Miller.*

'A few weeks ago you very kindly let me know that I might be asked to join the kirk session, and that this would involve eldership ... To be asked (if I ever am) to become an elder of Bonhill Church would be to present me with a very wonderful honour ... The reality of eldership is, I suspect, quiet, dignified service, requiring some sacrifice, much tact and the setting of a constant good example ... In fact it is all too easy to see my own unworthiness and unsuitability. I could fill pages with my inadequacies and doubts – perhaps I should. However, I am glad to say that my attitude towards this challenge has been coloured by the enduring memory of those many sermons that you have preached on the theme of the extraordinary things God can do with certain very ordinary people.'

I was enormously inspired by the following words written by Professor William Barclay:

When a man enters the eldership, no small honour is conferred upon him, for he is entering on the oldest religious office in the world, whose history can be traced through Christianity and Judaism for four thousand years; and no small responsibility falls upon him, for he has been ordained a shepherd of the flock of God and a defender of the Faith.

(*The Letters of James and Peter (New Daily Study Bible)*: 1 Peter 5.1–4, under the heading 'The Christian Eldership' – see Appendix 1.)

\* \* \*

By 1994 I was already active in other ways within the congregation, having been a Girls' Brigade officer and Sunday School teacher for just over ten years and representing both the Girls' Brigade and Sunday School on the Congregational Board.

*From the Urban Priority Area of Possilpark, Karen Ritchie writes of becoming an elder at a relatively young age.*

When asked to become an elder I was unsure. However, the minister at the time was very supportive and as there were a number of us in the congregation asked to join the kirk session at the same time a short course, led by the minister, explained the workings of the kirk session and the responsibility of serving the local congregation and the wider Church.

The main thing that gave me concern was that this was an ordination and was for life. I was still quite young and found the thought that this was for life daunting. I considered that I was already serving the Lord by my involvement in the children and youth work within the church, and that by becoming an elder this would extend my service in the local congregation as a whole and my part in looking after the people in my designated district. In that way I would also be serving the local community and wider work of the Church and thought that this was the way forward for me.

I prayed about it for weeks and read the Gospel of John and parable stories in the Bible on leadership. Some of these stories I'd known so well, like when Jesus washed the disciple's feet and called leaders to be servants. I got to thinking that this was possibly something I could do

8

in service to the congregation and community, and still think this in the eighteen years that have passed.

I would encourage anyone to become an elder as it has given me a wide range of opportunities that I would never have experienced before with the congregation and the wider Church. I also have grown in confidence and am able to share my gifts with other people.

\* \* \*

*Becoming an elder had not seemed like a good option to the young Muriel Armstrong.*

I suppose that becoming an elder was a natural progression in my faith journey, having been a committed church member for over twenty years previously. But I never thought I'd be an elder. Growing up as a daughter of the manse, I thought the eldership was something that got in the way – a kind of barrier in the church. I could think of very good elders but never thought I'd be one myself. In the end I became an elder because I was asked to be one, but I wouldn't have touched it with a bargepole when I was 20 or 25. And I don't think many young people think it's something for them.

I don't think I'm a particularly good elder but I like to do my bit – to get involved. I'm not 'holy, holy'. I don't speak the holy lingo. Maybe I ask too many questions – but I just think that sometimes we don't ask enough questions. I regard the whole thing as a journey – there are hills to climb, rivers to cross, hurdles to overcome. And I don't think we do enough questioning.

\* \* \*

*Two elders in Dunkeld, Perthshire, offer contrasting experiences of becoming elders. For Sally Robertson the decision took a great deal of thought – and the ride has not always been easy since. John Gray, however, moved into the role as naturally as a river into the sea.*

I've been an elder for four or five years, *says Sally.* When I was invited to take on the role, I recorded the pros and cons. On the plus side I had a huge sense of loyalty and love of the church – it had had a large place for me at key points in my life.

I was already part of the Mission and Education Group.

I'd also heard someone talking about being called 'kicking and screaming into leadership' and wondered if that was simply how it might be – responding to a demand.

The course I took answered some questions but raised more.

On the minus side there were theological issues that caused me concern, and I didn't think I had enough beliefs in doctrines to be an elder – for example around infant baptism.

There was the general church organisation, which I had concerns about.

There was the time required.

In fact, at one point, I did Google 'How do you resign as an elder?' – and, basically, you can't!

*Sally grew up in a Methodist family. Her mum was very involved with the Church – but Sally herself felt no sense of call. John doesn't think this at all unusual.*

The vast majority of elders don't feel any sense of call. They come into the eldership because of their background.

I was brought up in a very strong Presbyterian household. I had godparents; my father was the church treasurer (he was a banker with Clydesdale) though he didn't feel he was up to being an elder.

And my uncle was the Right Revd John Gray, Moderator of the Church of Scotland Assembly in 1977. Sunday was about Sunday School. Boarding School was the same – the weekly rhythm was built around church. I then taught in Sunday School.

It was just the way life was for us as a family. My father very influential in my life and I followed the same pattern. While living in England I was a member of a United Reformed Church congregation in Hampshire. The minister there became a very good friend; he was just a super person and he encouraged me in the eldership. It's about the relationships you have.

\* \* \*

*Like Sally, Graham Davie was not conscious of God's call in a clearly definable way.*

I had grown up with eldership in the family, my father having been an elder in another congregation for many years. The minister asked me and I said I would need to think about it. After some reflection and heart-searching, I realised that it 'felt right'. For anyone else thinking about becoming an elder, they will know if it feels right or not.

\* \* \*

*John Burnside was already working closely with his congregation's young people, and saw advantages for that work in becoming an elder.*

I was brought up in a manse and from that point of view, rightly or wrongly, I felt no mystique about becoming an elder. It was a logical progression and meant that, as Sunday School superintendent, I would have more access to express the needs of the young people in the congregation directly to the kirk session.

If there were conversations that moved me to view ordination as progress, then they were more likely to be those that resulted from frustration, feeling that the church needed to modernise and move forward as it was several decades behind the young people in the congregation; it was doing things out of habit rather than reflecting seriously and responding to changes taking place in the community.

\* \* \*

*Ian Maclagan believes that individual elders should play to their strengths. His words strongly echo the call for 'an honest appraisal of the gifts and callings of our elders' contained within the 2001 report to the General Assembly known as 'Church Without Walls'.*

The role of elder has to be revisited. Just assuming someone appointed to be an elder is going to be a good pastor is now an obsolete idea. We can't all be good at everything. Expecting someone appointed immediately to be a good pastoral visitor doesn't work. I would suggest that potential new elders assess and find out exactly what role they will be expected to carry out. No-one would say: we want to appoint you to be clerk to the congregational board even though we realise you are illiterate. (I realise that's an extreme example!) But in my humble opinion you don't try to put a square peg in a round hole. I think people should be appointed for their strengths rather than just because there's a vacancy to fill.

*'We need leadership. We need elders with vision and flexibility,' declared the authors of the 'Church Without Walls' report. 'The "one size fits all" pattern of districts is prevalent, but that does not give room for variety of abilities to be exercised ... Not all elders are gifted in leadership, nor are all gifted in pastoral care.'*

\* \* \*

*Beryl Smith is an elder in a remote, rural location in Shetland. A retired teacher, she is a Church of Scotland reader and acts as both session clerk and also clerk to the congregational board.*

For me, becoming an elder involved much prayer and thoughtful consideration, over a period of six years. I was aware that it was a great privilege to be asked and to feel that others thought I had something to offer. I was relatively young compared to those who were already elders, and they were all male. I respected them and thought they had seen more of life than me and therefore were more aware of the needs of the community. There was also a concern that women had not been involved in the elder-ship in our parish, and for many it was a difficult concept to accept.

However, I was teaching in the Sunday School and was in my own small way helping to form the Church of the future. I was also involved in transporting ladies to Guild meetings and in time it was suggested that I might as well 'come in'. I was immediately promoted to vice-president. The president then moved house and I became president – another insight into the workings of the Church.

For anyone considering becoming an elder I would urge them to pray about it, and if they have concerns on any point to discuss these with someone who is already an elder and whom they can trust to give them a confidential and honest opinion.

\* \* \*

Should I become an elder? *asked Winifred Thomson.* After much thought I felt this was the way forward – to be more than a member of the church.

\* \* \*

*John Macgill, who became an elder as a young man living in East Lothian, has mixed feelings about the role and how he was prepared for it.*

I've been an elder for more than 20 years. Why was I chosen? It was not done terribly scientifically. It was more a case of, 'Who can we get to be elder next – we've got some spare districts.' You need to prepare people for the eldership better than I was prepared. In some churches there's a huge investment of time in people being elders. Even in my late twenties I don't think I was necessarily well equipped; but, of course, you're flattered.

I lived in fear, when I was visiting members, that someone would ask me a theological question. In fact there were situations where people were in distress when I coped much better than I thought I would.

However, I don't feel comfortable with some of the formal occasions, for example when you're handing out the elements of communion – where you're taking on a role; setting yourself apart from the congregation.

It's difficult. You have a fabric committee that has absolutely the right people on it – architects, electricians; you have a social committee that can basically feed the five thousand; you have a finance committee that has the right people on it, who know about money. And then you have a session ... I think the session should be spiritual; to have that role supporting the minister in the pastoral and spiritual work in the church.

\* \* \*

I do not see eldership as conferring status within the Church, *says Alastair Christie-Johnston*, but rather as a way one can be of genuine help to the minister, sharing the pastoral role of caring for the congregation. I take note of the ongoing debate on length of tenure and believe that when one ceases to *want* to serve fellow parishioners in a worthy and meaningful way, then one should step down. However, this is not an issue of age in my opinion; it is one of love. An old man or woman may serve their church very well if they do it with genuine humility and in the knowledge that God is still with them. In my own experience as a youngster in my father's church, where latterly the session clerk was in his late eighties, I remember being inspired by that old man's obvious spirituality. His role as an active officer of the Church was undoubtedly diminished to the point of being virtually non-existent, but his presence at the communion table was a powerful testament to his love of God nevertheless.

\* \* \*

*John is an elder in the relatively affluent parish of Balerno in the Presbytery of Edinburgh, home to many professional men and women.*

There was one occasion when a member of my district was invited to become an elder and he was very reluctant to accept as he saw the kirk session as the place for professional people rather than tradesmen. He felt he would be out of his depth. I assured him he would be most welcome and that there were times when the professionals needed to realise there were other groups and perspectives in the congregation. He was forthright in his views and a good elder because he was committed to the church and to people. My advice would be to concentrate on people.

\* \* \*

You'd never find an islander volunteering to be an elder. I'm still of the view that if someone expects to be invited to be an elder, be very, very wary. I'd tend to question their motive. Is it because of the status? For someone to become an elder, others should see what is of worth in them; they should not see it in themselves.

We had gone down to Barra from Ness at the top of Lewis, which had a very strong Christian witness, *recalls Hamish Taylor, a Church of Scotland elder in the Western Isles for thirty-five years.* The congregation in Ness was very evangelical and everybody was highly theologically aware. The elders dressed in black on a Sunday and sat in a holy huddle in front of the pulpit. They were good, holy men and we felt a spiritual drawing. But as to making a commitment, though some very kindly people were urging us to do so, we made the island response: 'We're not good enough.' Those people were so good, they almost had wings on. I couldn't be like that.

*In Barra, at a distance from the sense of intense holiness that he had experienced on Lewis, Hamish now experienced a different kind of spirituality to which he felt he* could *contribute.*

Barra was different ... It's a predominantly Roman Catholic island and the relationship between the Church of Scotland and the Roman Catholic Church was very good (it could teach many others about working alongside Roman Catholics). I personally began to reassess where I stood. Barra was a place where even my witness could mean something. Would I be guilty of denial if I didn't make a commitment? I would be denying what I believed.

The thing I couldn't get away from was those words of Jesus in the Gospel of Matthew:

'Whosoever therefore shall confess me before men, him will I confess also before my Father which is in heaven.

But whosoever shall deny me before men, him will I also deny before my Father which is in heaven' (Matt. 10.32–33).

It was a challenge I couldn't get away from. By sending me to Barra, God had given me an opportunity.

So I became a communicant member there in Barra. And within a year and a half I was invited to be an elder.

# 2

# Promises, Promises ...

*Men and women who commit themselves to the role and tasks of the eldership each make a promise when they are ordained:*

> Do you believe the fundamental doctrines of the Christian faith; do you promise to seek the unity and peace of the church; to uphold its doctrine, worship, government and discipline; and to take your due part in the administration of its affairs?

*This vow is taken seriously by anyone who makes it and directly relates to membership of the kirk session. Since the times of John Knox, it has been the session that is responsible for upholding 'doctrine, worship, government and discipline' within a congregation and, where there is no other body, such as a congregational board, matters of administration also. But what the promise means in day-to-day life is sometimes more difficult to articulate. Responses to the question, 'What does the promise mean to you?' range from the emotional to the pragmatic.*

I hope and believe that the promise I made when I was ordained has helped me be conscious of the responsibility an elder has in caring not only for a district but for all of God's people. I think that when I became an elder it was in the hope that I could be a part of the vision for the future of the Church. I pray that the commitment I have for the Church and for God's work is in action as well as thought.

\* \* \*

*Isobel Alford has been an elder at Howgate Kirk in Midlothian for four years.*

I gave the promise a lot of thought and prayer. I had declined invitations to become an elder on two previous occasions because I was just not in a good place. So when the time came, and I was asked for a third time, it felt right.

I could have written a list of reasons about why I couldn't do it, but I felt God calling me to this. I realised at the time that I'd been called to Howgate Parish. It has a membership of about thirty-five and we regularly get up to twenty-five and sometimes more than that. But the first time I worshipped in Howgate Kirk there were thirteen people and I thought, 'God, you're having a laugh!' I'd have loved to go to a church with a choir – I love singing – and there are other places I'd have been thrilled to be but this is where I am. This was where God wants me to be and I know God will use me here. So when I took the promise, I was comfortable with it. I felt supported. Three of us were made elders on the same day. My family and friends came and there was a tea afterwards.

The language of the promise is very formal but I understand the meaning. There has to be a bit of translation involved. The first part I have no problem with. I understand the doctrines. 'Do you promise to seek the unity and peace of the church?' – that's a tall order. Fortunately I haven't been called upon to 'uphold the discipline'.

What difference has it made to me? My Christian commitment is there anyway. The difference is that I've committed to Howgate Kirk, the Church of Scotland and to the congregation. Beforehand I had less sense of being responsible for others, for members of the congregation. In making the promise we are taking our commitment to the congregation very seriously.

I have responsibility for the children's work in the church. We have very few helpers. And while I'd like to have passed on the baton to someone else, no-one was standing up to say yes. Had I not been an elder I might have said, 'To hang with it – it's time to move on.' But as an elder my responsibility is to keep on with this for the congregation.

\* \* \*

Being part of the eldership made me take my church membership more seriously and I feel responsible, along with others on the kirk session, for supporting the minister and caring for the congregation.

\* \* \*

*For John Gray, the heart of eldership, and the direction in which the Eldership Promise should lead any elder, is clear and straightforward. Yet he feels that many elders step back from engaging with it.*

Eldership is about evangelism! I was sitting in church listening to a sermon about the Thomas story *(John 20.19–31, which begins following the crucifixion of Jesus with the frightened disciples hiding behind locked doors).* And I wondered: why does the kirk session sit behind locked doors? We're frightened to reach out and speak about what we're uncertain about. But then, Scots are reserved. We don't ask about the business we're in, which is evangelism.

\* \* \*

In these troubled times for the Church, I believe seeking 'the unity and peace of the church' is paramount in congregation, session, presbytery, nationally in the Church of Scotland and ecumenically. I believe this is achieved primarily at a personal level and has to guide all our encounters with others. It is not peace at any price but I have constantly to relearn how to 'speak the truth in love' without being impatient or arrogant. My natural inclination is to walk away!

As a session clerk I have had to deal primarily with the 'administration of its affairs'. For me that meant dealing with paperwork as efficiently as possible and trying to respect other people's deadlines. However, looking out for people's feelings and changing circumstances has to take precedence where form-filling is concerned!

I think loyalty to session or congregational board decisions is of prime importance, irrespective of one's own thoughts. The temptation to grumble to one another is ever present!

I remember speaking to a session clerk who told me about her faith journey. She had no contact with the Church until after the birth of her first baby. One day she was pushing the pram past the open door of a church and felt an overwhelming desire to go in. She received a warm welcome and gradually came to faith. As an elder I was able to listen and encourage the telling of this story. It enabled me to marvel at a wonderful God who is constantly at work reaching out in ways we know nothing about.

\* \* \*

I was a member of the senior management team of one of the largest high schools in Edinburgh and I taught history. My beliefs and my involvement with the Church were known to all as, for some years, I led the Scripture Union group in the school. I did not proselytise and my belief was not part of the agenda for any conversation with staff or pupils but, at the same time, I did not avoid it when it was a natural part of a conversation or a lesson. Rightly or wrongly my personal mission was to present an honest but accessible line of communication for anyone who wanted to talk about beliefs, and to represent the Church of Scotland as being a user-friendly and understanding organisation rather than the caricature of John Knox and Rev. I. M. Jolly.

How do you measure the effectiveness of an elder? I wouldn't try in this context.

\* \* \*

With fewer and fewer ministers, the jam is being spread ever thinner. Elders have to be able to support the minister and do pastoral work. But not everyone can do this – it was never my forte. With hindsight, if I were asked to become an elder now, I'm not sure I'd say yes.

\* \* \*

I have been privileged to act as interim moderator now on two occasions and this has made the above promise more pertinent in my life

\* \* \*

*In the small congregation of Portnahaven on the Isle of Islay (though 'we don't think of ourselves as a small church'), Maureen Mackinnon's attitude to the Eldership Promise is straightforward and pragmatic.*

I was made the session clerk in 2001, just a short while after becoming an elder. It was because the lady who was session clerk was packing it in and she nominated me. The other elder seconded her of course. As you would. (There were only three elders at that time.) I had no say in the matter. It was the cards you were dealt. I was surprised. If you don't open your mouth quick enough it's taken as acquiescence.

A lot of our lives are like that. You have a loyalty. You don't want to be responsible for a failure. You don't want your church to close after hundreds of years. A great, great uncle of mine, Daniel Mackinnon, was a lay preacher when the church was built, at the same time as the lighthouse (*Rhinns of Islay Lighthouse, 1825*). So it's a commitment and I don't take it lightly. You made a vow in front of the congregation. It's that simple.

\* \* \*

*Alec Melville is a guiding light in the Bankfoot congregation in Perthshire. Talk of the Eldership Promise leads him almost immediately to reflections on the nature of kirk sessions.*

I find that in kirk sessions you've got the people who'll always say their piece, like me, and win their debate. And then there are a lot of others who nod their head then come out and say, 'We shouldn't be doing this.' Why?! I like people who call a spade a spade and say their piece.

I do what I do in the church because I feel God wants me to do it – but that links with the eldership because if I was not an elder I probably wouldn't be as involved. In the local community you've got to put something in. It's not because of the eldership that I get so involved.

\* \* \*

*Audrey Brown describes her experience at St Andrew's Parish Church in Arbroath.*

It's a responsibility around church to be welcoming.

There are about 200 on a Sunday and there's a worship opportunity on a Wednesday morning – about fifty are at that. And on Sunday evening there's a focus on modern music – it's targeted at younger people but there are very faithful older people who come along too. It's a very exciting place to be, but very, very challenging. It's sacrificial of time and talent and money. It has to hurt sometimes.

We're challenged to set an example and to try and encourage things like the house groups. It's generally an 'engaging' thing – getting people engaged in the life of the church.

We're constantly challenged in our church about promises and vows that we take, including, for example, during baptismal services, where we promise to support and nurture the children.

* * *

*Since moving church, John Macgill is not currently a serving elder but his memories of being one, and his experience of kirk session meetings, are strong.*

At the kirk session, spirituality hung up its coat at the door on the way in.

As a kirk session, we found ourselves involved in discussions about administrative matters where we had no more skill or right to be discussing these things than anybody else.

In our new town we have chosen to join the local church simply as worshippers. As an office bearer you can arrive at the door and find yourself waylaid about problems people are trying to work out. Not as much time is spent devoted to worship as to worrying.

What puts many elders off, in my experience, is the legalistic stuff. If you told many elders that the kirk session is the first court of the Church, they'd be hugely alarmed. The term elder was appropriate for a different age. The idea of the minister being the presiding elder ... it's all very warm and nice but it's just an anachronism. The session should be there as a spiritual support mechanism for the church rather than as a first court of the Church or an exclusive group.

Interestingly, though, I went to a lovely service at our new church where three members joined. I was really pleased for them. Then all the elders stepped up to welcome them. I wasn't one of them so wasn't allowed to, and I felt disappointed. I wondered what it must be like to be in a church for most of your life and to have been neither invited or chosen to be an elder nor allowed to welcome new members. The whole point of Presbyterianism for me is that nobody is more important than anybody else. There's only one person we're answerable to and that's God. On the one hand it's nice to have that bit of importance and to be able to welcome the new members; on the other hand, how interesting that it *mattered* to me that I was not allowed to do so.

\* \* \*

Is the promise something you think about very much? Not daily, no, *says retiring presbytery clerk Ian Maclagan*, but I did once have occasion to remind my fellow elders about it. When we were short of money! Giving your time and talents is a very Presbyterian thing. But I'd be telling a lie if I said I gave it consideration very often. I suspect very few elders consider what their obligations are on a daily basis.

\* \* \*

I am a hands-on person in the main and I love being involved with lots of different areas of church life. I often find myself trying to be a good listener (and remembering when this should be kept confidential), and in contrast to this working hard when I need to say something that challenges or disagrees with the argument.

\* \* \*

The Church of Scotland has around 40,000 elders – an enormous resource. It is time for a 'national audit' to assess the quality and commitment of this resource – particularly in regard to the spiritual dimension of the eldership. They all make a promise, and quite a serious promise. But how committed are they and what are their views?

\* \* \*

I was already taking note of the points of the promise before becoming an elder. I think all members should abide by the tenets of this promise, not just elders.

I seek to be welcoming to others and to listen to what they have to say. My hope for the Church is that it will return in deed as well as in word to upholding the Bible as the supreme standard of life and doctrine. I think in that way that the peace and unity of the Church will follow.

In personal story terms, I have felt more in pursuit of my calling as an elder since I retired from (paid) work and have much more time free to give to the Church. As a retired teacher I have been able to use my skills in helping a few people to read or to improve their reading. Anyone of course could do this – you don't have to be an elder – but sometimes being an elder gives an overview of what might be required at a given time.

* * *

The eldership is not as I imagined it. It's a much more positive experience than I expected it to be. Which is positive!

* * *

Being aware of other people's wisdom is important. Coming into the session, it was mainly middle-aged and older people – I came as a young person. The love that was shown; they wanted to share it with you – they invited you in, gave you confidence. I had a lot of difficult things going on at the time and they just took me right in, just in the way they were. It was almost like a father passing on gifts to his son or daughter – it was about sharing love.

# 3

# Seeking Spiritual Growth

*In a report brought to the General Assembly of 2003,
church members were invited to 'rediscover the full significance of the eldership as a spiritual office'. However, the
daily realities of being an elder often raise questions around
the interplay between the life of faith and the people and
situations encountered by elders as they undertake their
duties. Several speak of the sometimes painful challenges
to personal faith that arise from a tension between deeply
held beliefs and the need to engage with those who
express very different viewpoints. There is rarely a clearly
definable sense of cause and effect between being an elder
and experiencing spiritual growth. Some elders speak of
a precisely opposite effect or identify other areas of their
church life where that growth is far more evident. Nevertheless the importance of maintaining a spiritual life, and
the impact of prayer and reading scripture, is always recognised and frequently motivates eldership activity.*

\* \* \*

*Graham Davie has been an elder for just two years in a
congregation within the central belt of Scotland.*

I've probably been 'challenged' rather than 'grown' since becoming an elder, due to becoming aware of tensions and divisions in the life of the congregation through attending the session and business committee. There are some quite unhappy situations, which you would not have expected in a church situation.

*Similarly, another elder speaks of* a very sad thing, but I find my faith has been challenged by the acrimony that can prevail within the Church – something I was less aware of before I became an elder.

\* \* \*

My prayer life and meditation on scripture are fundamental to my life as a Christian. If people do not think this way they should decline becoming elders in the Church.

The Church is the Church of Jesus Christ; it is not just another organisation or social club. I need to be in communication with God in order to make decisions, to see the needs of others, to have time for them and not selfishly pursue my own way or ends.

To be an elder involves being willing to listen to others and to God and to forgo one's own idea in favour of another who is clearly receiving and understanding what needs to happen next. Strife in a congregation is usually as a result of office bearers who don't understand the responsibility of service but instead wish to pursue some idea of their own regardless of whether it blesses the congregation and honours God or not.

\* \* \*

*Alec Melville's sense of how important it is to nurture the spiritual life began when he was a leader in the Boys' Brigade.*

There was always a spiritual thing there. I was always very, very aware that you have to have a spiritual aspect for the boys. Going to church now I'm not holier than thou. From time to time I say I want to get more involved in prayers, reading the Bible ... But I realise that I haven't done this, I haven't done that.

\* \* \*

I realised that while many of the tasks I performed in the church were not spiritual, there was a spiritual dimension in sharing my faith, visiting people, offering hospitality and using my talents for the church.

When visiting my elder district I was sometimes asked, 'Why?' This caused me to study my Bible more in order to meet the challenges I face during my visits.

During a presbytery meeting an elder sitting behind me said that in his area they were unable to have services as they had no-one to lead them. That smote my conscience as I had taken occasional services, usually with the Sunday School pupils, but had refused to countenance training for the Church of Scotland readership. So after prayer and reading certain verses in the Bible, I agreed to train, and within months I had embarked on readership training. It was quite demanding but certainly encouraged a lot of growth in biblical theology and background to faith.

Regular Bible study is now an important part of my week. Using others, where possible, in sharing faith in the

Guild, in church services and in study groups enhances the life of the church and the lives of those involved.

\* \* \*

*Hamish Taylor, however, has mixed feelings about the impact on his faith of being both an elder and a reader. In 1994, he and his wife moved back to Harris from Lewis. Not long after, the Presbytery of Uist organised a conference on the island – an occasion that led Hamish to an important realisation.*

I wasn't a member of the Presbytery of Uist at that point but the presbytery clerk asked me if I'd speak about the role of the laity in order to set the theme for the day. After I'd spoken I asked for questions and one minister stood up and said, 'You are an elder. And also you're a lay preacher. Do you think these two roles should be centred within the one body?' I couldn't answer. I apologised and said that I would think about his question. But that evening the answer came to me very quickly and I phoned the minister that night. I said that if I was a reader first and then was invited to become an elder, I'd think about it. But being an elder now, and knowing church politics like I do, if I were asked to become a reader I wouldn't touch it with a bargepole. It would take somebody with quite a strong faith to be involved in both areas of activity.

*More recently, Hamish has moved to a new congregation on Harris where he does not have responsibilities as an elder or as a lay reader.*

For the first time in thirty years I've been able to sit

beside my wife in church, listening, taking in the Word, without worries about governance and politics intruding, and that has been a wonderful thing.

\* \* \*

*Donald MacKinnon was the first elder-moderator of the Presbytery of Argyll (*'a challenging but memorable experience'*). He is a regular worship leader and conducts funerals.*

On most Sundays I am conducting worship, either in my own congregation or elsewhere, and this would be impossible without prayer and reflection

\* \* \*

Hopefully my faith has grown as a result of being an elder, *adds Hamish Taylor.* Maybe that's for other people to judge, not me. I hope I'm aware of following what scripture says. But I've also been a reader since around 1984. Because charges were vacant more often than not, a number of us became readers and that's when quite a lot of us grew spiritually. We were preaching a lot and were experiencing first-hand what it meant to be part of the priesthood of all believers. This was a medium of growth for me more than being an elder.

\* \* \*

I find that reflection on scripture has led me to believe that the Bible is a very complex and difficult collection of books, *says Willie Scobie, for whom Bible study is an important part of his life as an elder.*

These books were written over a period of several hundred years, by many men with differing backgrounds and purposes. They may have been inspired but they were human and fallible. The Bible's meaning, or meanings, are by no means always clear. Accordingly, I suggest, the Bible has to be very cautiously interpreted.

Many very clever, spiritual and qualified people have come to significantly differing conclusions about aspects of the Bible. Within the Church of Scotland a wide range of views are to be expected and respected. Ultimately I have come to believe that each one of us has the awesome responsibility of finding our own interpretation of scripture. Usually we will resort to some 'authority', but at the end of the day it is the individual who decides whether and precisely what to accept, and from whom. This, of course, opens up before us the terrible danger of embracing that which comforts us and rejecting truths with which we are uncomfortable or incapable of accepting.

\* \* \*

My inclination is to say that my faith has grown *despite* being an elder. What I *have* experienced is more to do with my relationships with other members.

I don't think you enter into the eldership with the expectation that you are going to get a lot out of it. I was doing it because I was giving something back.

\* \* \*

I believe my faith has both grown *and* been challenged through eldership, *says Alastair Christie-Johnston, recalling a period when he lived in Tasmania.*

Initially I undertook training sessions and attended conferences designed to equip me better for the role, and through these I gained deeper faith. Later, when actively serving in pastoral care, I met with people whose faith was much greater than mine, which challenged me to rethink things. In particular, early on in my eldership I met a young couple who had suffered a painful bereavement and I was inspired by the way they coped with the tragedy. Through them I learnt something of the power of prayer to bring about acceptance and understanding.

Around this time I also met with a professed atheist who demonstrated a fuller knowledge of scripture than I had and used it with devastating cunning to cut the ground from under me on more than one occasion. I realised then that faith founded on ignorance was little better than a house built on sand. I determined to become better informed and enrolled in a three-year correspondence course in theology.

At the time, the only college offering a course of this sort was one run by the Anglican Church of Australia. Completion of the course led to my becoming involved in lay preaching, and for the next five years I had full responsibility for a small rural parish in which I conducted weekly services and officiated at weddings and funerals. Once again I found myself more ministered to than ministering, and frequently wondered at my own presumption in taking on the role.

* * *

Because I've been a spare elder (without an assigned district), occasionally my mother has called on me to do some visits around her districts. I'd met one gentleman who – and this was a tremendous privilege – then asked to speak to me at church one day. We became aware of people listening to us and so we got out and went to a coffee shop. The situation he spoke to me about I could easily have responded to by saying, 'Don't be ridiculous. Your relationship with God is far more important than a promise to another man.' But I listened to him, a west of Scotland man, knowing that when a working-class male makes a promise it is an important thing. And he felt so much better for having spoken about it.

All I did was give him space to speak. But he suggested that ministry might be a possibility for me. He said it was unusual for someone so young to hold back and just listen. So now I've started on a period of 'Extended Enquiry' (investigating the possibility of applying for the Church of Scotland ministry).

* * *

I find it hugely difficult to unpick my faith story and attribute elements of growth to my specific role as an elder, but it's a good question!

I think my early experience of eldership led me to believe I had a role in leadership of the local church, and being a young, zealous evangelical Christian I was keen to engage people (primarily those that I visited) in meaningful conversations about faith. I was also aware in those early days that my role was pastoral and practical, so it sometimes involved hospital visits, attending funerals and picking up shopping.

Most of my professional life over the last twenty years has related in some way to scripture and theology. I have experienced early certainty, then an almost complete loss and deconstruction of faith, followed by a reconstruction (slow and wonky yet real).

I now serve as an elder in a conservative-evangelical church where I would like to think I offer help and encouragement to those with questions and doubts while engaging with those on the fringes. I try to do this in a way that is honest and not 'subversive', not least because at heart my faith is predicated on Christ as my saviour. My understanding is that Christ saves me from myself and my need to be in control. This sense of control extends to being better than other people, being more moral and self-righteous and being able to garner God's favour and thus get into heaven while enjoying some good old idol worship on the way!

Having just recently attended the General Assembly (*of 2013*), this understanding of my own faith journey really helped me get a sense of what is at stake (in my opinion) in relation to the issue of clergy in same-sex relationships.

\* \* \*

I have made it a priority to pray regularly for those I visit as a district elder – the prayer that God would bless them and that they would be aware of his love for them. Members who do not attend church are a particular concern. Sometimes they share with you the reason for this; sometimes they don't. One lady did return to church and became a faithful attendee after the death of her husband. This encourages me to keep praying for the others. I believe that God is reaching out to them in ways I will never know, and attending church again is not the only indicator of the Spirit being at work.

My faith as an elder was severely challenged when I was a presbytery committee convener and I encountered people who were more interested in legalism and their own specific agenda than working fruitfully together. I believe that as an elder you have to receive from the Lord before you can give anything. Prayer and reflection on scripture are essential to this. I also believe that you have a special responsibility to pray regularly for the minister and other leaders in the congregation. Probably this should extend to presbytery and the national Church too, but that aspect is less regular!

* * *

*Katherine Shaw, a retired teacher and community educator, offers an excellent example of an elder who is hugely involved in a wide range of activities in the life of her congregation – as a president of her Church of Scotland Guild, a member of the pastoral care group, a Young Church leader and as convener of the flower committee.*

I naturally prefer to be doing practical and creative things. But of course being still or prayerful is all a part of being very practical. Getting the balance right for my own well-being is important. Maybe that is where acceptance and contentment are. And maybe that is where the energy needed to 'do service' comes from.

* * *

Despite experiencing the power of prayer in others, I cannot claim to have found dynamic uplift for myself through this means of grace. Rather I gain a sense of inner peace and wait for something more. In this I acknowledge a failing on my part that I equate with lack of faith.

I am constantly being enriched by thoughtful preaching and consider myself blessed to have known many fine ministers. My own reflections on scripture also continue to help me grow into faith, and I believe both make me better able to serve effectively as an elder.

Now in my seventies I recognise that my faith is to some extent more intellectual than spiritual, and for this reason I value more than anything else the unquestioning faith of many good kirk folk I have met along the way. My best friends are Christians.

# 4

# Experiencing Change

*How has the role of elder changed over the years? What are the perceived challenges from society at large to the way the Church organises itself? What are the new challenges for kirk sessions? Some experience of change for elders has arisen from a new awareness of their role as charity trustees within their local congregations, resulting from the establishment of the Office of the Scottish Charity Regulator (OSCR) following commencement of the Charities and Trustee Investment (Scotland) Act 2005. (See footnote on this matter in* Eldership in the Church of Scotland, *p. xiii.) Many elders are also especially alert to evolving legislation relating to safeguarding and the protection of vulnerable groups. Others reflect on changes in lifestyle and commitments that impact on the way they can carry out their eldership duties.*

Being an elder was different from what I thought it was going to be. You rarely feel called upon to respond pastorally, and most of the time you're relieved because you don't think you can do it. There's no shortage of things to do but they are administrative things. You can easily find yourself very busy but equally, well, I'd thought there was going to be a greater spiritual dimension to it. In a way it's what you make of it, and I'm not necessarily convinced that being an elder makes it easier to do things.

\* \* \*

*Muriel Armstrong is an elder who would welcome more change.*

In our congregation the role of elder has not changed in any way. We still have communion cards that are delivered to our districts quarterly. There are better ways of monitoring the membership and freeing up elders' time.

\* \* \*

There was a wee bit more respect in those days – reverence – when the elder came to the door. The public at large – if they think of an elder doing his or her duty at all – simply thinks they're trying to do something; getting involved in the church. I'm not sure you get so much respect today. It's just one of those things you don't really know. You can try and try with people all your life, visiting, and then – bang – something happens. It's about communicating with people and helping them relax.

\* \* \*

*Hugh Paterson, a former session and presbytery clerk, believes that the heart of the elder's task is still to get up alongside people; not just the church members in the district but everyone in the district. But he has seen a broadening out of the tasks undertaken by elders, in particular when his congregation was without a minister.*

Elders who are able to, take church services. From about 2003 to 2009 our charge was vacant. We had a dedicated reader but even so the interim moderator was scrambling around to find preachers for each Sunday. Latterly, three or four times, elders led worship. It's amazing how needs must.

*(More thoughts about elders leading worship are included in Chapter 7: Making Some Things New.)*

\* \* \*

In 1968, when I became an elder, there were loads of young elders at that stage, *recalls John Gray, currently elder in a largely rural parish in Perthshire. Asked about elements of change in his experience of the eldership now, he is blunt:* There's lots of pushing and shoving to get churches to come together and it's a complete nightmare.

\* \* \*

I've been lucky always to have served under ministers who were trying to find the best and most inclusive way to get the best out of the people who were on the kirk session. Church life has evolved but not changed necessarily. There are many more younger people, younger parents, on the session nowadays – the spectrum is there from people in their thirties to their nineties – so it evolves because older people can't commit to the same extent and young people come in with new ideas. And I've been lucky that ministers have encouraged new ideas.

\* \* \*

The social set-up has moved on, *says John Gray*. Women are working more and so on, and there are so few young elders. Life is different now. *One of his colleagues on the kirk session in Dunkeld is Sally Robertson, who speaks for many younger people as she describes balancing her commitments as an elder with her work and family life.*

I was at a meeting of the kirk session recently. I compared the way mobile phones have developed over the past ten years with the lack of change in this church. What do you think people said? There was no comment! Nothing at all. I couldn't work out what people were thinking. It left me wondering if people are committed to the change required to stay in touch with all members of our community.

At age 46 I'm the youngest member of the current session. There are about thirty-six on the session – around twenty turn up to a meeting. The next oldest among us is probably in their mid-fifties. I don't always make the kirk session – I'm usually on the run, taking the boys to one of their clubs. Sometimes I just forget. I am aware, though, that we prioritise what we want to prioritise. Reflecting now I wonder whether, if the session spent more time focused on the needs of our community and world and less on maintaining what we have, I'd be more likely to get to the meetings.

I find that the structure of our session meetings works against discussion. We sit in two rows in front of the minister and session clerk, who sit behind a table. I'm used to sitting around tables so I can see the people I'm meeting with. I think we need to set ourselves up to encourage greater participation. I have recently asked the session to reconsider the way it sits ... I'm waiting to hear what people think!

*Sally believes there are real opportunities to be had in the area of Dunkeld and Birnam, which her parish covers. She describes the Birnam Institute – extensively and imaginatively enlarged as part of a local millennium development.* It contains everything – a library, community classes, ballet classes, a ceramics room ... The school uses it for end-of-term events. I think it provides a really interesting model for how the church could be.

Achieving change – in a community this size – is difficult because you don't want to fall out with anybody. And change is hard anyway. However, I am prepared to keep trying.

* * *

Prior to coming to my present church fifteen years ago I served in my previous church (in another Christian denomination) as one of twelve elected leaders. The leaders were appointed by the church congregation. The length of service was four years, at which time the person stood down or, if willing and asked, would stand for a further four years. The members of the congregation would cast their votes, determining the outcome.

Is this a future model for the Church of Scotland to adopt? I question the idea of 'once an elder, always an elder'. It is not unusual for elders to leave a congregation for a variety of reasons, yet they continue to remain an elder. I believe, in the not too distant future, as old age and passing away comes our way and sadly we lose elders, that many of them will not be replaced. The kirk session as we see it today will be restructured to suit the ever-changing shift throughout society.

\* \* \*

*Hamish Taylor speaks of his experience in the Western Isles.*

I think elders are expected, on Harris anyway (because we are relatively few in number – and particularly as presbytery elders), to be more involved in Church politics than an elder was in my early years. Back then it was the minister who did the 'politics' – but they were very straightforward then. Today, Church politics is as much a minefield as any other politics. Elders have to do it because the ministers are snowed under by their proper work.

\* \* \*

I find the creeping legislation to which the Church is exposed both a threat and an opportunity. A threat in that the legislation can outweigh the spiritual calling – it is easier to fill in forms than trust God. But it's also an opportunity in that it gives increased openings for good training where reflection on all aspects of the role is offered.

Personally, I dislike the legislation around safeguarding because at heart I feel it should not be necessary for those called by God to a task in the Church. However, I realise that this is considered naive in our present culture, given the church examples of child abuse that have become public of late. I have to admit that legislation has proved necessary.

\* \* \*

It used to be the case that an elder was ordained with a primarily spiritual role as the constitution of most congregations sought to distinguish between the spiritual and the temporal through its courts and committees. Latterly it appears to have become the case that part of the role of the session – and therefore the elder – has been hijacked by the need for congregations to comply with recent legislation regarding charitable status. While it is no bad thing for congregations to show due diligence in the handling of their affairs and to record their dealings, it is a major distraction from spiritual activity and needs to be recognised as such.

I have had dealings through my occupation with issues of child protection and safeguarding. The modern default setting is that we start off with a presumption of ill intent. It is the nature of a serious paedophile to find ways around the safeguards – whatever they may be. Do we have our safeguarding processes in society (not just the Church) to protect our consciences as much as to protect our children?

These two paragraphs perhaps illustrate a disillusionment or cynicism. Every church has to operate within the society in which it functions and to reflect the concerns and manners of that society. Our society has changed in the last fifty years and is generally more selfish and more cynical and, in some ways, as an organisation we have to compromise. However, we need to remember that despite these changes, the most important thing is the individual relationship with, and faith in, God and fellow human beings.

I find that sometimes I do have to distinguish between my relationship with God and my relationship with my church. I have not always felt thus.

\* \* \*

I think the safeguarding programme is essential. Our congregation embraced the idea of safeguarding from its earliest inception. I am not the safeguarding officer but I serve on a very small group that oversees safeguarding in our congregation. Elders should be aware that there may be vulnerable people among us and see that they are being properly cared for.

Being a trustee is a serious responsibility. Elders need to be aware of what is going on in order to fulfil their responsibility. Attendance at meetings is a duty and is important. These responsibilities are to be taken seriously and people who do not understand the real meaning of these changes need to wake up and see that they carry out their responsibilities diligently.

\* \* \*

Safeguarding and the protection of vulnerable groups (PVG) is a sad reflection of our present time – particularly in churches, viewed through the ages as 'places of safety and refuge' and now proved otherwise. It is essential that vulnerable groups are protected, and crucial that appropriate measures are in place to maintain their safety. As elders we have a duty to protect our elderly and our children, and I welcome legislation, training and good practice to carry out this duty.

\* \* \*

Perhaps it is true to say that it could be considered a 'concern' to be a trustee, since most church members own their own homes. *(See footnote on elders and liabilities in* Eldership in the Church of Scotland, *p. xiii.)* However, it should lead to more 'openness' on the part of the accountant/treasurer/financial committee, and afford more involvement and commitment of the kirk session with regard to making financial decisions on behalf of the church.

\* \* \*

*Sue Allan was ordained an elder on the Isle of Gigha over twenty years ago.*

This is a small community and though at the time the membership of the church was slightly higher than it is now, there were only three elders and the session clerk was also the treasurer. Our present session clerk and I were ordained at the same time, and since I have a reasonable ability with figures and had experience as a treasurer with the local village hall, I offered to take on the treasurer's job, which I have done ever since.

I haven't had any formal bookkeeping lessons, just some really basic stuff when I was at horticultural college. What I found difficult was that, nearly every year, there seemed to be something different to do in the formal accounts that had to be prepared for 121 George Street *(the Church of Scotland administrative offices in Edinburgh, known as '121')* and the presbytery. To a certain extent things are easier now that we have to prepare them for OSCR as the format stays the same each year, and using a computer spreadsheet helps!

We were very wary when OSCR first arrived on the scene, but last year I went to a conference to meet OSCR in Oban and found that they weren't the ogres we had thought them to be but people willing to help with our problems and actively eager for us to get things right! Although there have been other courses held for treasurers over the years they have usually been at places a long way from the west coast! I have to say, though, that I have usually found those I have spoken to about the accounts at '121' very helpful.

\* \* \*

*A perceived change in the role of elders is their position as trustees of the Church of Scotland. Retiring presbytery clerk Ian Maclagan says that, in fact, this is nothing new.*

Elders have always been trustees – they just haven't realised it! It has been forcibly brought to attention in recent years with the establishment of OSCR and other legislation. Personally, if I felt the trust of which I was a trustee was not being properly administered, I'd resign. (Being trained as a solicitor and having sat as a sheriff, I'm well aware of the implications of being a trustee! Many elders, however, are not.)

Where I have seen a change is in the sense that elders are having to become of much more assistance to ministers. The role of the elder thirty or forty years ago was to deliver a communion card three or four times a year and to attend the kirk session. Now there are elders in the Presbytery of Argyll routinely conducting public worship or funerals and acting as interim moderators for congregations where there is a vacancy. Elders are very much more 'professional' in their job. Twenty years ago you'd never have found a presbytery clerk being an elder – clerks were one hundred per cent ministers. But we had an elder-moderator in Argyll last year. There simply aren't the ministers to go round. More and more, elders and congregations over the years are going to have to be good at DIY.

# 5

# Hopes and Dreams

*How elders describe their hopes and dreams for the future often says a good deal about the concerns and challenges they face now. In identifying opportunities and naming aspirations, another unspoken question arises, which is to what extent elders themselves are in a position to effect changes to make dreams and prayers reality. Clearly, in many instances they are in such a position – most frequently in identifying needs in the communities around them. And while there is a desire for numbers to be present within church on a Sunday, there is an equal if not greater concern to find ways to respond to those wider community needs and build relationships with neighbours and potential partners – by enacting the Christian gospel.*

I hope that we make far better use of elders. There are over 35,000 of them – someone called them 'a silent army within the Church'. If you turned round to any organisation and said, 'You have that number of volunteers signed up for life: what will you do with them?', what would they say?

\* \* \*

I think our congregation is welcoming and friendly to newcomers. I would hope that in ten years' time we are still the centre of our community – but perhaps with a much younger kirk session.

\* \* \*

*In Oban, Donald MacKinnon dreams of 'mission to the un-churched'.*

Our congregation tries to put God first and to have him at the centre of all we do. We seek to share the gospel with the community and all who come into church. I think we are friendly and welcoming because people who come in tell us we are. We are not stuffy traditionalists but we *are* God-centred and Biblically based. We want to welcome people and have them feel at ease.

In ten years' time I hope there are even more people from the community attending church and feeling a part of it. I would like to see more groups bringing people together and making them feel welcome and supported.

I believe social life is changing more and more quickly and so the church may well look very different by 2023. Perhaps we may meet at different times in the week to worship, as well as on Sundays.

\* \* \*

Through the week our halls are filled with folk of all ages, coming in for classes or activities with every imaginable title. In contrast, the number participating in regular church attendance is small. As a church we do reach out and many events are successful, but we really need to note the fact that many hundreds of folk come through our foyer door each week – happy, energetic folk, most of whom have no idea what the inside of the church looks like, let alone what it feels like to be inside on Sunday at a service! Taking stock of this must be the key to the future. At present we have two full-time ministers, both very energetic people. But they are not connecting in any way with all these folk. I would love to see them connecting and involving themselves through the week in and around our foyer and halls.

My hopes for ten years away would be that we know each other better, are more supportive of each other and that we look outwards to areas where there is need – and that we do something to improve that need, either in this country or abroad.

\* \* \*

*Andrew Kimmitt speaks of his hope that the Church of Scotland maintains, and works with, the Third Article Declaratory. The articles declaratory of the Church of Scotland's constitution (enshrined in Scottish law in 1921) define its structure, form of government and membership details. The third of these articles acknowledges the 'distinctive call and duty' of a national Church 'to bring the ordinances of religion to the people in every parish of Scotland through a territorial ministry'.*

We've moved past the possibility of having one minister in one parish right across Scotland. But there's something poetic and deeply right about the idea that wherever you are standing on the soil of Scotland you are in the embrace of the Church of Scotland. The question is, how could that be done in an ecumenical manner? It's not necessary to be doing it in the same way as in 1560 (at the Scottish Reformation) or 1929 (the union of the United Free Church and Church of Scotland). The ministry of the Church of Scotland needs to be something more ephemeral – not necessarily something that happens on a Sunday morning.

It has a huge role to play in an independent Scotland, if that's where we're going. For instance, already it is bringing a visionary role to the care of people society is not willing to take care of. I would like to see more visionary work around mental-health issues.

\* \* \*

We are a priority area congregation situated in the north of Glasgow, *says Karen Ritchie* – fifteen minutes from the city centre. We are a welcoming and friendly congregation with many ageing members still doing what they can to serve their church and community. We serve the community well with our weekly activities. The church also gives access to many local community groups, such as a credit union, Kinship Care Group, Narcotics Anonymous and Alcoholics Anonymous.

My hopes for the next ten years are that:

- We still flourish as a congregation within our ever-changing community and offer a place of hope and support to those who need it.

- We begin again our youth ministry and build on our relationships with the local schools.
- We have a new health centre across the road on vacant land that has been empty for over thirty years so there may be something we can also offer the community, with a possible healing ministry.
- We support the work of Faith in Throughcare, which supports ex-prisoners returning to the community to stop reoffending. One of the things we are considering is supporting the ex-prisoner families and offering a space for them to meet.

\* \* \*

I would describe the congregation at my church (at Auchincruive in South Ayrshire) as 'welcoming', *says Pat Johnston*. However, we are a very small congregation at both churches, so we decided to ask the local community where they felt a) there was a need and b) how best to address that need – in terms of elderly people, single parents and young people. With the assistance of staff from Priority Areas Glasgow we, as volunteers, have almost completed a training course and are now arranging to meet again with the new recruits and church members from the North Ayrshire Groupings to discuss further the way forward.

I hope that in ten years' time we have a drop-in centre/ lunch club for the elderly, a progressive parents and toddlers group and a youth group, offering a range of activities and opportunities.

I also hope that we are viewed by the community as a church that has 'reached out' to embrace the needs of the people of our community and, by working together, achieved our aims.

\* \* \*

I suppose my dream, really, is for more outreach to the community. For example, for years the United Church of Bute has run a Pass It On project. We rented a shop where we stored furniture – beds, cupboards, kettles and so on. But we had to stop because we couldn't afford the rent any longer. We now have a store of basic essentials for people who were homeless – 'starter packs'. It was sad that the furniture store had to be curtailed but this is more manageable.

\* \* \*

Our quinquennial review revealed that we were all of a mind to do more outreach. When and what is the need? We don't yet know – you have to get to know people, and people need to trust you first. We're not called to convert our community to Christ. We're called to deliver the gospel to our community. God will do the rest. I feel we should be doing, not talking.

\* \* \*

*Anne Shaw, an elder in Balerno in the Presbytery of Edinburgh, paints a picture that many congregations will recognise – of many years' development of older buildings to make them viable and appropriate for mission within the local community. The benefits, she suggests, are sometimes won at more than just financial cost.*

Our church has been responsible for quite a few community initiatives. I would describe the congregation as vibrant and active. We have the advantage of being in the middle of Balerno and therefore visible. The Mill at St Joseph's (a new café) is a huge success, bringing in non-members both as customers and helpers. I am aware a great many people involved are over 60 and 70 and there will be a gap when they can no longer manage the hours of involvement. However, there is good attendance by young families.

In ten years' time there will be a need for taking account of the elderly.

I hope we shall still have a minister and an emphasis on spiritual as well as social activities.

I hope we don't rely too much on visual presentations and can continue to hear good sermons.

I also hope we will be off the treadmill of fundraising, which has been going on for one building or another for the last thirty-five years. These have been the new hall, a replacement for the manse because of dry rot, the removal of pews and complete renovation of the church, and then the development of the St Joseph's Centre (the former Roman Catholic Church next door, sold to us when they no longer had use for it, and now the home of our café). There *has* been a positive side to all the fundraising in that it brings people together. It can also be divisive.

\* \* \*

*Sally Robertson explains that an unusual arrangement in Dunkeld means* we have two active church buildings for a congregation of eighty, plus a manse, the Chanonry and the Duchess Anne church halls. The cost of maintaining so many older buildings means there has to be a lot of fundraising. For example, the kirk has recently joined with the Episcopal and Catholic congregations to set up the very successful 'Three Churches Charity Shop' to raise money to support the various churches in the village. I am concerned that the need for this maintenance diverts attention away from what we do for the community – for our young people.

\* \* \*

We have two morning services, which tends to divide the congregation, although there is the opportunity to meet for coffee and so on between services. Quite a number of members have left due to differences of opinion with certain parties. Hopefully in time some will feel able to return.

\* \* \*

*Sheilah Steven's concern and vision centres around the difficult issue of a proposed church union.*

Our congregation is lively, friendly and served by an outstanding minister. The worship is outward looking, challenging and varied, and there are lots of activities for all ages apart from regular times of worship.

Our presbytery ten year plan states that we have to unite with our neighbours Lenzie Old. However, they have appealed the plan, and nothing can proceed until either their minister or ours demits office. This is not a happy situation and means we have to look at our mission solely in terms of Lenzie Union at present. Buildings will be a problem as no resolution about which are to be kept can be made until the Lenzie Old appeal is heard or when either minister demits.

In ten years' time I would like to see our congregation perhaps leaner but fitter to reach out to the community in creative ways and be a faith-nurturing presence for all connected with it. The journey to get there, at present, seems tortuous! However, difficulties do tend to produce faith.

\* \* \*

We hope we can just keep going, *says Maureen Mackinnon from Portnahaven Parish Church, a proudly maintained parish church in the far south-west of Islay.*

We hope that we will never close. When I was a teenager and there were only twenty-five people in the congregation, people said it would close – and it's still here. It hasn't changed very much over the years. More people are moving into the village. They think it's a pretty village, buy a property, but have nothing to do with the church. They have use for the church at times but they're not really interested. They come from a different culture. Commerce is rife outside the temple!

\* \* \*

*Winifred Thomson is a former bank clerk and has been an elder for twenty years.*

The ways of the world have changed so much these past years. We have to move on or, as a church, we will stagnate. I would like to see more people in middle life being part of the church.

\* \* \*

*Like Maureen Mackinnon, Hugh Paterson has also served as an elder in the largely rural Presbytery of Argyll. A former international banker, he hopes for a time when we make better use of our resources – a vision he acknowledges many find hard to share when push comes to shove.*

We all know there are too many churches and too few ministers. I'm sure the costs are getting out of hand. I'm afraid I feel that the Trustees (of the Church of Scotland) are too soft. People from the head offices in Edinburgh would come to visit a rural congregation who were looking for £50,000 for a new roof. The next Sunday they'd go to another congregation who needed £20,000. And they're saying 'yes' to it all. Meanwhile in Inverness, Glasgow or Edinburgh there are congregations paying for it all. Why don't these smaller, rural congregations get together under one roof?

Presbyteries won't make it happen. If an elder stands up in presbytery and says, 'We need £50,000 for a roof', it's 'Yup – OK' ... because they all know that next month they'll be making a similar request to deal with woodworm. You can't trust presbyteries to make these decisions because they have a vested interest. And it's the wealthy congregations who are paying for all this. In Argyll there were four congregations that were aid-giving. All the others were receiving. They'll never be self-sustaining.

\* \* \*

By and large I think the traditional idea of Church is going to change drastically. I think the remit of an elder having a district and undertaking pastoral visits will change. There will be fewer church buildings. (Is that a bad thing? Not necessarily. We may not have the silly situation of five churches within 500 yards of each other.)

If you want to encourage growth you've to clear out the dead wood. I think we're going through such a period of clearing out. And that will leave us with a leaner, stronger kirk.

I think there's a great deal of enthusiasm and energy from young people. But there's resentment too and the need for resilience to be able to bounce back from that. And that resilience will only go so far.

\* \* \*

I guess my hope and prayer is that the Church of Scotland will survive in this area and it will continue to be regarded as the national Church in our country. I suppose I have specific ideas of how that will happen. We have to be far more open to others and place outreach at the heart of what we do, rather than be inward looking.

# 6

# The Elder as Pastor

*Some elders will be assigned a group of members on the congregational roll with whom to keep in touch. It is a task rooted in pastoral oversight. Often such groups of members are organised on a geographical basis, hence the term 'district elder'. Traditionally visits were also tied to the routine of delivering communion cards – invitations to attend communion on particular Sundays in the year.*

*Two striking ideas come through these accounts by elders (some of whom also make the point that pastoral work is not appropriate for every elder). The first is that elders frequently 'receive' more than they offer in pastoral situations, learning about themselves and growing in their faith. The second is that taking the pastoral duty seriously may involve making painful decisions or lead to radical, even controversial, actions.*

The biggest difference I experienced when I became an elder was that I gained access to people's homes! I got to know people better than perhaps I would have just socially. Occasionally I had to get a minister to visit. A minister won't know if someone's in hospital unless they are told, so it's up to the elder to tell them. Ministers don't always visit, but I think they should give the customers what they want.

* * *

An older couple joined our congregation when their previous congregation was united with another and our church was closer to their home. They had been very active in their previous congregation but it had become harder as they aged. They became regular attendees with us, and the wife, as well as delivering the church magazine, joined the Guild and participated in all the activities until she gave it up to care for her husband. I remember when I first visited them that she said, 'Will you say a prayer for us?' That became a regular part of my visit. They were devoted to one another.

When the husband died his wife was devastated. They had no children but a nephew invited her down to his home for weekends and she was unable to attend church any more on a Sunday. It took time but first I encouraged her to attend our short Wednesday-morning service and she found some comfort there. At first she found going to our regular Wednesday-morning coffee shop difficult as she was on her own and there seemed to her to be a lot of couples there and other people who knew each other well. However, she persevered and became part of that too. I started to take her out for lunch regularly. The time came when she no longer needed to stay with her nephew at weekends and she returned to Sunday-morning worship with us. She is now one of our most faithful members, always has a word of encouragement for others and takes a particular interest in those who haven't been to church in a while!

I see my pastoral role in that situation as being an accompanier. In the early days I wondered if her faith would desert her, such was the level of her grief. However, I am thrilled that she is now such a great witness to God's faithfulness and such a blessing to others. In many ways this 'rehabilitation' was a team effort and a number of people contributed to her healing, not just the elder!

\* \* \*

There have been several occasions when I have been in a situation of providing support and hopefully comfort to the bereaved. On the first occasion the deceased had been a close friend and I had to ask myself, 'Am I doing this to help the bereaved, or am I doing this because it helps me?' The honest answer on that occasion was a bit of both, but it made me think subsequently that pastoral support is not about dropping in to say what you think is important, it is about listening for what the bereaved person feels is important and responding to that. Everyone is different – you can take nothing for granted and there are times when there is nothing you can do to make it better.

\* \* \*

There was a married couple I visited in my district. Both died of cancer, one a year after the other. They were so brave. I would like to think that visiting them made me a more understanding person.

\* \* \*

I had a district at that time – there were a number of families for whom I had responsibility. Visiting involved talking about family matters, including where there was a family break-up. I'd be calling in, listening and, if asked, would refer a matter to the minister or other agencies. This was normal, ongoing pastoral care, I'd say.

\* \* \*

*Audrey Brown says that her experience of being widowed at a young age has made an impact on how she offers pastoral care.*

My husband had long, long periods of illness. There were a lot of crises. Through that I was given increased understanding and patience to listen to others. And in the choices I had to make for my husband and our two children, I had to have a sensitivity raised in me for how to be with other people. And that has stayed with me in my work as an elder.

\* \* \*

*Some elders tell stories that involve very serious, sensitive and sometimes deeply personal situations. It is clear they can find themselves in positions of considerable responsibility and worry. This may lead an elder into a difficult place of conflict with other elders and church representatives.* I felt under huge pressure to let matters rest. I was accused of pursuing a personal vendetta ... *wrote one elder, who nevertheless felt that deep pastoral concern had brought him to this place and that subsequent events justified the actions he had taken. It becomes clear that, even in less serious cases, pastoral care is about far more than making a visit and sharing a cup of tea.*

I grew up in my church and when I became an elder I was very worried about visiting my district. Sometimes it is harder to share your faith with folk who have known you as a child. I visited an old lady and asked if we could pray together. As I left, she hugged me and said, 'Thank you for helping me speak to God.'

I had on one occasion to visit a family whose son had been murdered. It was difficult and I felt so worried as I knocked on the door. Can I say that I was warmly welcomed as '(M) from the church'?

I had prayed before I went that God would help me say the right things. I really didn't say very much, but holding the parents' hands, they knew I felt their pain and we were able to pray a short prayer for strength.

\* \* \*

I've only just been given a district, *says one young elder who was ordained aged 26.* For two years I was floating spare, though I'd sometimes cover other people's districts. And, yes, someone did say it was because of my age. I was very frustrated by that. Other people not much older had a district. I wanted responsibility. The job that I do (as a support worker for adults with learning needs) means I have to be a people person – I *am* a people person. I want to get in and serve people.

I was given a district and I went round to visit this gentleman I'd always thought was rather cold. And I saw a totally different side to him. I'd judged him to be this type of person and I shouldn't have been judging him in the first place. Within five minutes I realised his wife had dementia and he was caring for her.

We talked and he said to me, as a new district elder, 'Here's my advice to you ...' I wouldn't have expected that from that gentleman. Yes, of course I was willing to listen to him. I think you have to learn from other people. There's no one way of doing it.

\* \* \*

It's the spiritual dimension I find hard to get involved in, *admits Hugh Paterson.* Maybe two or three times in twenty years I was asked to pray in the house I was visiting. Maybe I should have offered more. I don't know ...

\* \* \*

*As a new elder, Jamie Stuart shared that concern but found that having a few simple techniques to hand helped him in such situations.*

In my early days as a Christian I reckon I was always a wee bit apprehensive (or scared) of presenting a prayer in the company of others.

I do believe that the late William Barclay helped me

to have confidence in this direction. He wrote to the effect that when we are (or were) speaking to our father on earth, we would speak naturally and with confidence and conviction. We should act the same way towards our father in heaven. Very often elders feel that their prayers must be as eloquent as trained preachers.

I decided to take William Barclay's advice. I found it extremely helpful to start a prayer to a single member of my church district, or to a group meeting, by, first, thanking our heavenly father for all the blessings we have in this world *before* requesting help for other blessings. Only after expanding on all the joys this world has to offer do I request blessing, comfort and hope for all the peacemakers in the world and for the poor, needy and bereaved. I find that way is very easy for me and should be for any elder.

\* \* \*

For a good few years, along with a friend, I have been responsible for driving a lady who is elderly and blind to church on a Sunday. Doing this task has given me insight into the many difficulties she faces. I much admire her courage and resilience. Over the years she has become even more determined to attend church, though we do, on very snowy days, find ourselves persuading her to stay at home!

She has helped me realise just what an important part churchgoing plays in our lives. I know she is a strong person but she has grown spiritually stronger in the time I have known her, and somehow I guess that much of this comes from her weekly contact with church worship or with the fellowship of people who take an interest in her, and from the fact that she is in the later stages of life.

\* \* \*

*Hamish Taylor speaks from the distinctive experience of living in the Western Isles.*

I exercise a pastoral role most obviously at times of bereavement. People lean on you because even the funeral directors here have a different role from on the mainland. Here they just do the practicalities of the funeral. Elders have to organise the pre-funeral services – prayers in the home and also on the evening before the funeral itself, usually in the church.

We have a big role in helping the family smoothly through the proceedings. It's a hard enough time anyway, but funerals here are quite culturally embedded and when families feel that the proceedings have to conform to cultural expectation, that's a lot to deal with. So elders come into their own, carrying the family, and this implies a deep knowledge of local genealogy. We know our families very well! This is important, for instance, because of the order in which people stand around the coffin. The most senior member of the immediate family stands at the head of the coffin and the next most senior at the foot, and then you go from one end to the other with three people each side. And there are a lot of relatives on the islands! One lady in Helensburgh rang me on Harris and said she'd like me to arrange her husband's funeral. She said she'd prefer me to do it, having known the family. The local minister didn't know the family because he lived away.

\* \* \*

*Donald MacKinnon recalls:* As an interim moderator on the Isle of Tiree, I was asked to sit with my senior elder as he died. While this was a daunting task, I felt it was also a tremendous privilege and felt the presence of God with me at that time.

\* \* \*

*Maureen Mackinnon's first language is Gaelic. There is a pastoral quality, she suggests, in using a person's first language. It helps start a conversation and build a rapport.*

I'm a Gaelic speaker and that is very useful if you have to go to someone's home with the minister, say, and they only speak English. When you speak in Gaelic to one another, it's not confidential – there's no posing about it. But you relax in it. You can say things and you've got the understanding – it's your first language. You can start a conversation in Gaelic and then continue on in English. I can deal with older folk who are happy to explain things in Gaelic.

\* \* \*

My district started as sheltered houses but changed to houses for people over 50 with housing needs. This changed the whole feel of the area and was difficult for the elderly people already there. More of the residents are non-churchgoers now. The warden service was removed.

As I had been on the committee of the Housing Association for many years, I was able to approach them to ask if they could be more sensitive to placing less disruptive new residents. We had had incidents of attempted murder, drunk and disorderliness and drugs. Two different residents had to be evicted. All this was extremely alarming and unsettling for the elderly people, some of whom had lived in their houses for many years.

I was widowed at a young age and find I am able to empathise with the members of my district. It was quite hard thirty years ago but I suppose experience and age help. All my original district members have died but I know the current ones well.

I am careful not to become too involved, as long as there is family support, but I find my members talk to me about family worries and their own concerns. I have been able to help them in various ways or refer them to someone who can.

I have always considered it a huge privilege to visit my district and to be welcomed to their houses. Sometimes when life is busy it can feel like a chore, until one gets there, and often I have come away much enriched by the experience. We also have a good laugh!

\* \* \*

*Muriel Armstrong is unsure about the value of delivering communion cards four times a year to members of her district, but she does perceive pastoral value in a simple practical task that she carries out with others.*

There's a hazy idea about elders being pastoral. I've found that the only people who open the door and invite me in are the people who come to church anyway. The one person on my list whom I've never met has not been to communion in twenty years so far as I know. Some of the older people ask you in and you chat with them. I think they see you as their channel of communication to the church. But I do feel, when I deliver communion cards and then people come, just four times a year – I think, 'Why?' It puzzles me. Are they simply maintaining their place on the roll?

I've actually got a very small district. One of my old ladies went off to stay with her daughter. Another old boy died. He was actually in a nursing home for years and I was part of a group who went to pick him up and bring him to church on a Sunday. This was organised by our pastoral group. Now I'm part of another group doing that for someone else – this is for people who have been stalwarts of the church, and I think this is very important. It's really a pastoral role worth carrying out.

\* \* \*

Make a point of talking to people. At communion time I go round every house in my district and invite them to the communion service. You don't get in every house here compared with when I was in Paisley, say. There it took ages to get round; you'd go round and have a good old chat with tea. In Bankfoot, mostly there isn't the same kind of opportunity … I miss getting in to be a wee bit closer. Sometimes there's a question that I can ask, like 'How's your mum?' That's often the only way you can get in.

\* \* \*

Pastoral care is a core part of the task of being an elder but I think it can be done better. The problem with the model is that it is not really there for pastoral care. A lot of the people involved are expected to be good at pastoral care just because they are an elder. It's like asking a teacher to go and be an engineer, or vice versa. It makes sense to be using people with a strong pastoral sense as well as elders – using them *both*.

\* \* \*

The role of the elder has changed considerably in the area of pastoral care. In the past, each elder was designated a district and was responsible for visiting congregational members within that district. The purpose was to ensure they were looked after, for example driving people to hospital appointments or to visit partners in hospital.

The districts in question are now covered by members of the church, their remit being to deliver the church magazine and dialogue with those to whom they are delivering. As a result, information gleaned can be passed on to the church pastoral coordinator and any necessary action can be implemented.

\* \* \*

Being a 'newbie' on the kirk session I avoided the devastation created within our congregation by a very difficult situation that resulted in a minister leaving. There was real hurt – and it's still there. This is many years later. In dealing with that very serious event, the elders of the kirk session had to draw together to deal with the fallout and overwhelming sense of loss. The needs were both spiritual and also practical, for example arranging who would lead worship for each Sunday.

* * *

*In recent years, the sharply reduced number of ministers on the islands and the increasing number of struggling congregations have persuaded Hamish Taylor, an elder in Harris, to exercise his pastoral role in a radical way.*

There was a question in the air because of the General Assembly decisions (over the status of ministers in same-sex relationships) – a question as to how people would react to that. Some people have left the congregation because of that. Others intend to. I'm not sure that on its own the issue would have pushed me out. But for a couple of years we have formed a very close relationship with the Free Church congregation in Leverburgh. We would have a prayer meeting once a week on a Wednesday and also the Free Church was having a prayer meeting on the very same evening. So the question arose: Why couldn't we share a prayer meeting once a month? Our minister was sent to ask the question of the Free Church minister and it turned out that, on the very evening we had been discussing the matter, the Free Church session had been discussing the same thing. Was that human coincidence or something stronger?

There's less and less sense, to my mind, for two small, struggling congregations in the same community deliberately to continue to stay apart. Not only does it make human sense to join together; I wonder whether it doesn't also make Christian sense.

*Hamish's deliberations have led him to take what he regards as a lead and move to the Free Church congregation, where he now worships each Sunday. He describes this as a pastoral action – demonstrating what can be possible and hoping others will understand.*

It's difficult for many people to see it the same way as me. I thought that, as elders, part of our role is to lead and to pastor the congregation and, if necessary, lead the congregation to where they can get the best pastorate. And, from my own experience, it is in the Free Church. I have made my move out of pastoral concern for the congregation; I find it hard to see the Church of Scotland congregation surviving even in the medium term.

* * *

I don't think elders simply fit into a single category, *says retiring presbytery clerk Ian Maclagan. He argues that not everyone is suited to pastoral work and shouldn't be forced into a single mould of elder.*

We all have different talents. I'm not a good visitor – it's just not my forte to go and visit people. My strengths are in my administrative abilities. I've been forty years as an elder. For ten of those I was the Session Clerk in Rothesay. When five of our churches on Rothesay united, I became interim clerk to the Session and Clerk to the Board. For ten years I was clerk to the Presbytery of Dunoon. In 2004, the Presbyteries of Dunoon, Lorne and Mull and South Argyll united and I was appointed as clerk to the new Presbytery of Argyll. I got the new presbytery up and running – it was a mammoth task. But I'm not a district elder. When I became a session clerk I said I couldn't be a visiting elder in Bute – which suited me fine.

* * *

*Some congregations appoint elders to specific roles that do not involve care for a district. Graham Davie, an elder in a busy suburban church, is one example.* My role is as a 'business elder' and I have not been called on in a pastoral situation.

* * *

There have been individual instances as an elder where I've visited people – and I was always a reluctant visitor – and sometimes I thought, 'Am I doing any good at all?' when people answered the door and it was a polite 'Thank you' and that was it. But there were a few occasions when I blundered in when people were in distress. The role I was fulfilling any member of the church could have done, but being an elder gave me the confidence to do things or to say that this or this was a good idea.

My experience is that the congregation knows exactly how to support the rest of the congregation. And there are those who are particularly skilled at doing quiet work in the community – some of whom are elders and some not.

In a perfect world you do not need a group of elders to be able to reach out to the community on behalf of the church. There are two dangers of setting aside a group of people to do that. The first is that you might be tempted to think it's sorted because you've mentioned it to an elder rather than doing something yourself. It's difficult. We're Scots. We don't do unrequested help very well.

Second, there is a risk that if you create this group of elders you create a barrier between the congregation and the minister – a layer. I'm not sure if one was to design a new structure that we'd come up with this one.

# 7

# Making Some Things New

*One person's innovation is another's habit of routine. A tiny change for one congregation may have huge significance for another. Context is all, as the following comments illustrate. What becomes clear, however, is how often innovations are down to the passion or drive of an individual elder rather than the vision of an entire kirk session.*

*Alec Melville is an elder in the small village of Bankfoot in Perthshire. His story tells of a clear sense of call, a long wait and then a moment of radical opportunity. It begins with Alec's early retirement following a career in insurance.*

We were living in Paisley and wanted to live in Perthshire but couldn't sell our house. At that time the Presbytery of Paisley sent round a circular to each congregation about the areas we covered, wanting to change the parish boundaries. This was fine. There was a new part of the town that we could take in very easily. But then the presbytery decided that it wanted to shut down our existing church and send us into another area altogether. I became a spokesman in our congregation, saying 'no'.

So we had this big meeting with the presbytery and during that the congregation won its case. We wouldn't move. After the meeting was over I was driving home when I suddenly heard this loud, booming voice: 'You can go now.' It was that clear – a really clear voice in my car. Two days later, the house was sold.

We moved to Bankfoot and friends asked us, 'What are you doing going to a wee, hicky village?'

We had been in the village for about eight or nine years and then, on 25 February 2004 – Ash Wednesday – the old church burnt down. Everyone was in shock. It wasn't just a fire inside the church – the whole thing burnt down. It had been the centre of the village – the clock chimed away every hour. There was a real grief in the community.

Nearly all the locals said they wanted a new church to go back where it was. It was that idea of it's 'aye been'. But I thought, 'What an opportunity!' The thing was, the old church was up a hill in the middle of the village and there was no road access – you couldn't get a car up there – and it was a steep climb for pedestrians. It was surrounded by a graveyard and so you couldn't build out either. It had the only church hall for the village, but that wasn't big and couldn't be extended.

*The congregation was in a vacancy at the time. Supported by its interim minister, the Very Revd Dr Jim Simpson, the congregation searched for a new minister, who turned out to be a minister just coming to the end of his time as a naval chaplain, the Revd Iain McFadzean. His vision became one for a new church building down the hill, better able to support the church's mission and enable partnerships with many other organisations within Bankfoot to grow.*

There was a real stramash in the village. But the aim was to serve the community – and this was a really pragmatic approach. Letham St Marks in Perth offered a model to work with, and we approached the architect and building firm who had worked on that.

We had an opportunity for the year and a half we'd been without a minister. Everyone had mucked in; things got done. It worked extremely well. In that interim situation there was real potential for the elders to kick in. We couldn't just sit back – we really had to pull our weight. And now I became a kind of spokesman again. The new minister had the vision but needed a great deal of support, someone with a thick skin to act as a backup for that vision. It turned out that was me. That voice in the car that had said, 'You can go now.' It had boomed out. I felt that God had put me in Bankfoot and I didn't know why. I was waiting for nine years. But the fire took care of that; it answered my question. I knew, 'This is it'.

*The opening Sunday in the new and impressive Bankfoot Church was on Sunday, 26 October 2008. Alec Melville remains a leading light within a congregation he, as an elder, helped lead into a new way of being. The full story of the journey from the Ash Wednesday fire to a development of a new church and community complex is told in* A Building Vision: Bankfoot Church and Community Building Together, *by Ian McFadzean, available from Bankfoot Church Centre.*

\* \* \*

Being now over 60, I look at some initiatives with a degree of scepticism and sometimes concern, but I reflect back three decades and remember when I was frustrated at the fact that the Church did not seem to be moving with the times. My role is to challenge but not to oppose, and to support by getting involved when I can.

\* \* \*

*Willie Scobie's examples illustrate the value of each individual bringing his or her passion and skills to the development of new ideas and initiatives.*

Some years ago I started up an Amnesty International Support Group within the congregation at Bonhill Church. About six persons were involved and we played an active part in several campaigns that resulted in the release of prisoners of conscience. Each year, around Christmas, I address the congregation of Jamestown Church and invite them to send messages of support to prisoners of conscience and other victims of human-rights abuses. Usually we send between fifty to sixty cards, and occasionally replies have been received from the prisoners themselves. I have been doing this for around a dozen years.

In 2006, at the request of my minister, I wrote a short history of Bonhill Church and Parish. The money generated by sales of this was donated to Teen Challenge, a Christian-based organisation that very effectively helps young people with addiction problems.

\* \* \*

Our session is very supportive of schemes that we believe are necessary in Urban Priority areas and that cause us to trust God in faith for financial provision for these. As a session we seek to encourage the congregation that a food bank and a Christians Against Poverty (CAP) centre that counsels and supports those in debt are necessary.

\* \* \*

*The vision for the Havilah project began to emerge at St Andrew's Parish Church in Arbroath in 2006.* It came about because it was a church looking forward, *says Audrey Brown.* We were a parish church and next to us was a homeless unit. There were a great number of people in difficult situations, dysfunctional families, real poverty and addictions.

There was talk about a mother and toddler group for young women but it was felt that something larger was required. A drop-in that catered primarily for people with addictions evolved, initially on the church's own premises.

There were tensions to work through. Originally we met in the church halls and there was a bit of friction with our 'traditionalists' in the congregation. Members of the congregation were coming face to face with people they didn't understand – they were a bit intimidated.

It was a gradual thing – very much about growing, learning, caring; all these things. I felt, as an elder (I was the session clerk at the time), that my task was about encouraging people to hold in there. People interested in the project were often younger – very new Christians.

They almost demanded action straight away. I had to temper it and say, 'It will be in God's time.'

*Havilah now operates from its own premises nearby. Many members of the congregation are involved in all aspects of its work, including providing lunches.*

Volunteers who make soup (about thirty of them) are all from the congregation. Part of my remit as a member of the session is to inspire and make a spark for those who felt this was not for the church, and help them get back to Jesus' message, 'Truly I tell you, just as you did it to one of the least of these who are members of my family, you did it to me' (Matt. 25:40).

*Read more about Havilah on the Church of Scotland's own website in the Go For It Fund's 'Stories of Change' section:* www.churchofscotland.org.uk/serve/go_for_it/ stories_of_change/articles/havilah; *or on St Andrew's Parish Church's own website:* www.arbroathstandrews. org.uk.

\* \* \*

*Through leading worship, elders often find themselves trying things they haven't done before. They 'step up', making pragmatic responses to situations in which they find themselves. What is the norm for one congregation may be quite new for another.*

We are part of a linkage, which works very well, *says Maureen Mackinnon, an elder in Portnahaven Parish Church.* And we've just got a new minister after a three-and-a-half-year vacancy. We all kept going with no drop in the congregation in that time. Our hearts weren't in our boots or anything like that. We had some locum ministers and other people wanted to start a worship team. I was leading worship occasionally – I don't drive but I said I would do it in Portnahaven. I still do it – I've led worship with the new minister. During the vacancy we worked from a book, using starters from the computer because we're not qualified. We chose hymns according to the readings, and prayers of course. And I was keen on marking Sea Sunday: we're an island, the sea is important, you have to acknowledge it. We're keeping the church going. You just do what any other church would do.

* * *

Since returning to Shetland almost four years ago I have been involved in attempts to revitalise a declining parish where the average age of members is over 70. The parish is spread over three islands and includes five separate congregations, all struggling to survive.

The congregation with which I am chiefly involved is that of St John's, Mid Yell, where we have a weekly attendance of ten to fifteen, four of whom are elders. At 73, I am the youngest elder and the youngest member of the congregation is 60. My wife is the organist.

The logistics of bringing worship to the people of Yell is nothing short of ridiculous. The Church of Scotland has three churches on the island – one at the north end, one at the south and St John's in the middle. Besides this, weekly services are held at an Episcopal church at the south of the island and at a Methodist chapel four miles further north. Four of the five island churches are within ten miles of one another. The number of different preaching places makes it impossible for our minister to cover all of them every Sunday and so worship groups, consisting mainly of elders, regularly conduct services in his absence.

I have accepted ('assumed' might be a better word!) the leadership role in this for St John's congregation and have the full cooperation of the others in doing so. We adhere to the lectionary and, by and large, attempt to follow the established form of service used by our minister. Due to our sermons being shorter than the minister's we usually sing five hymns instead of four and occasionally use the extra time to learn a new hymn from Church Hymnary 4 *(the most recent Church of Scotland hymn book, published in 2005).*

As the church is large, draughty, uncomfortable and expensive to heat, we have successfully persuaded a reluctant-for-change congregation to transfer worship to our kirk hall after undertaking some low-cost and mostly superficial redecoration and adding the inducement of a cup of tea at the end of the service – provided the hour is suitable.

Worship Group services have been held at various times, eventually settling on 11am as most suitable, while those led by the minister are of necessity either at 3pm or 6pm.

A 'Yell Churches Together' committee has been formed, ostensibly to bring about greater cooperation within the denominations, but it appears to lack the intestinal fortitude for honest-to-goodness unity. Most of its effort amounts to little more than window dressing, but I admit it is early days and it is a step in the right direction. In truth, no-one wants to be the first to close their church.

* * *

We use elders to deliver 'community prayers' (prayers of intercession). This may not be that innovative, but it is so far as my previous church attendance is concerned. I am involved in this initiative on a regular basis.

* * *

There is a definite move at St Andrews Church (in Arbroath) to use the ministries that members through-out the church have, involving individuals from all age groups, for example in holiday clubs, the welcoming committee, Messy Church and so on.

The elders are still responsible in assisting the minister in the act of communion, serving the bread and wine to their fellow congregational members.

The church objective is to be a community-based church. This involves volunteering church members, some of whom are elders, getting involved in activities outwith the church, for example in paired reading in the local Arbroath Academy, working with Havilah – an organisation set up by the church to help those addicted to drugs and alcohol (*described by Audrey Brown above*) – and providing 'starter packs', which involves giving out food to those in need.

* * *

*John Macgill's experience of being involved with two congregations has led him to reflect on the symbolism of serving communion in two different ways.*

In church A the elders take the communion elements of bread and wine first and then pass them around. In church B the elements are passed around the congregation before the elders themselves are served. I didn't think this mattered to me, but having seen it the latter way, it just feels right. Actually, elders are the ones who must always put themselves last. Where being an elder was once a mark of seniority, this way of doing communion says, 'We've recognised your activity in the community and you will go last.' Ideally, that's what we're doing as elders.

\* \* \*

*Innovation can come through learning from the experience of others – other churches and other denominations.*

We now have two services, and the one at 9:45am is geared towards families, though a lot of older people go. There's a praise band at this service and more contemporary music, and the children are there. Everything is done from the floor – there isn't a sermon from the pulpit – and a story is told that links in with the Sunday School curriculum. Interestingly, more people go to that service than to the second one with organ music and a more formal style.

I'm on the worship committee. It only meets once in a blue moon. But on Sunday a few of us are being sent out to go and look at other churches – to see what they do and ask ourselves: 'Should we be doing this?'

\* \* \*

Recently I dropped in to St John's Episcopal Church in the West End of Edinburgh for their one o'clock service on a Friday. The service was taken by a lay member. A beautiful service – simple and easy to be a part of, with a communion that was a simple laying on of hands and anointing with water blessed by the service on the Sunday. I came out into the busy street much refreshed and strengthened by the experience, and I wonder whether it is time to open our own church doors through the week.

\* \* \*

*For Hugh Paterson, living a in a rural area, pragmatic ecumenism has become the norm. He speaks of the unusual situation on the Island of Colonsay, in which circumstances have resulted in a committed and dynamic Roman Catholic acting as session clerk to the local Church of Scotland congregation (there being no Roman Catholic church on the island for him to attend). Hugh's own experience, in the congregation of Kilcalmonell near Tarbert, is equally telling.*

When I joined there was a membership of about ninety. It's now about forty but, strangely enough, the worshipping congregation each Sunday is about the same. Many of those who move into the area are from other denominations – Anglicans or Congregationalists ... We've even got one Roman Catholic lady who comes every Sunday. And we don't make any distinction.

I remember, at one time, looking around the congregation and there were more there who *weren't* members than were. We wanted those people to be part of us. But if you're a Roman Catholic or Anglican, you don't want to give up the faith of your birth but want to be part of it still. So we invited them to be adherents and now we have ten adherents. This has strengthened the life of the congregation.

* * *

*Too often shared ideas get forgotten, Muriel Armstrong feels.*

We have an annual conference as a church. I'm afraid I'm a bit cynical about this. We divide into groups, we answer questions and someone takes notes and reports back. Our thoughts and ideas are written up on a flip chart. But then the flip chart goes back in the drawer from whence it came. And you ignore what you've discussed and simply move on.

* * *

We're trying to get a skate park set up for the young people, *says Sally Robertson from Dunkeld. Her own children are keen skateboarders.* This is about me using 'my voice'.

I have a car with fuel. It would be easier to take the boys to Dundee or Perth. But I think there is a real issue of villages investing in young people. So I'm trying to understand what they want and help them but I'm doing this without support of the kirk session. We've had conversations but it's too hard. I feel I'm doing this as a response to the call to the Church to respond to the needs of young people. We need to be seen to be supporting outside community groups actively and reporting back to the session.

I call meetings but I'm very opaque in fronting them. I don't say that I'm calling this meeting as an elder of the kirk session. No-one would come. The kirk session cuts no ice at all.

# 8

# Making Space for Young People

*As churches endeavour to engage with children and young people, they find themselves battling against prevailing social trends ('the opportunities for other things on a Sunday morning are enticing'). There are those who believe it has ever been thus. Traditional methods of offering church-based activities for young people (Sunday School, the uniformed organisations, summer clubs and so forth) remain standard. Are there other ways of building relationships with young people, and can elders play a role? Fresh ideas are not abundant in the responses from elders that follow, though a number of supportive organisations are named and attempts to invite young people into positions of leadership may point to one way forward.*

In our congregation we have a Sunday School, which includes children from two to sixteen years. *Speaking from Dunrossness, Shetland, Beryl Smith describes a typical range of opportunities for young people.* Over the years the numbers have varied from four classes, sometimes, to one. We used to have one teacher per class, but with legislation around safeguarding now in place we ensure a minimum of two adults to each group. Often mothers will accompany their very young children after attending the first part of the morning service, which all children attend.

We also have a group for teenagers after church on a Sunday evening. That group is ecumenical. Apart from weekly activities, the group is involved in music and sometimes leads worship, as well as being asked to entertain at local events.

The Girl Guide movement is strong and attends church for Thinking Day and Remembrance Day. There are also three sections of the Boys' Brigade and they meet every week during the winter months.

\* \* \*

I have always worked with Sunday School, *says Katharine Shaw, an elder at Fairmilehead Parish Church in Edinburgh*. At Fairmilehead it is called Young Church. The main change I see is in the attendance, both in numbers and pattern. We have a small number who come regularly but the opportunities for doing other things on a Sunday morning are enticing! So we are lucky that we do still have a lot who will also come back to church occasionally. Being creative in how we keep or encourage them to keep coming is crucial.

In the summer holidays we do run a holiday club – we've done this for maybe three years now. A large number – almost one hundred – come every day for five mornings. And on the Sunday following, they come back into the church and show the congregation what they did. The adults who help love it and the children do have a wonderful time. But the numbers it actually brings to the Young Church is tiny in return for the week provided.

I know about Messy Church and I know that its concept and ideas are being taken up. The fact that it involves parents as well as children appeals to me. I am hopeful that we will be able to run one or two pilot Messy Churches in the future.

*Messy Church is a form of church designed primarily for children and adults who don't already belong to another form of church. It is built around a creative mix of activities, celebration and hospitality. You can find out more about this initiative from the Messy Church website:* www.messychurch.org.uk.

\* \* \*

As a congregation we employ a full-time youth worker. As well as assisting our Girls' Brigade, Boys' Brigade and Sunday School he is involved with Scripture Union in the local schools and Urban Saints (*an evangelical organisation, formerly known as Crusaders, which reaches out to children and young people* – see www.urbansaints.org). He also runs youth events. Many youngsters are around the church who have no church connection at all.

Along with the Episcopal and the other Church of Scotland congregation in Lenzie we run a one-week summer holiday club for children and teenagers. This year a number of teenagers who had grown up with the holiday club took on significant leadership roles, which has to be good news! We also have a Millennium Fund which provides financial support to those engaging in Christian work overseas, and this year a seventeen-year-old went to Brazil to help in a project working with shanty-town children.

We have a children's 'orchestra' for nine- to sixteen-year-olds who participate in the first part of morning worship.

On the downside we have increasing difficulty finding volunteers to work with young people, but we are indeed blessed to have so many around the church.

\* \* \*

Older people tend to be wary of the youth, *suggests one younger elder, now aged 28, who reflects on why so few young people are ordained as elders.* They think, 'Oh, they'll come in and change everything!' But, actually, if there's only one younger voice, that will be very difficult. They're forgetting that many of them were young when *they* became elders.

There's not a history of passing on the baton in the Church. In our congregation we were in a right mess when the treasurer died. It was no great surprise – the gentleman had been in his seventies. But there was no-one to take over. Folks get into a job and do it for thirty or forty years and so young people think, 'That's *their* job.'

On the other hand, there was one kirk session meeting where the property convener, who had been doing the job for eight years, said he was going to retire. Another elder stood up and said he was doing a good job and should stay. 'No, no,' said the convener. 'That would be wrong of me to deprive someone else of the opportunity to do

God's work in this way.' Until someone steps back, you don't know who will step forward. People need a push towards it.

\* \* \*

*A number of elders perceive that engaging with young people is about growing a congregation that values all-age activity; that understands what it really means to be a 'church family'. Audrey Brown speaks of her experience in Arbroath and Anne Wanless of efforts being made in Wester Hailes, on the outskirts of Edinburgh.*

I think we've been fortunate in our minister, who was a young man when he arrived (in Arbroath). He was very keen, very organised, very reflective. He had an old head on his shoulders so that he took people with him. The session was made up of middle-aged to elderly people at that time but all the discussions were very constructive. It was a very patient ministry. So we have church family days – it's not necessarily all about youth clubs or Sunday club: a church meal, perhaps, or a church barbecue. The thing about being a family church is that it has to be *real*.

Of course it's also very generational here. With the fishing families of the town, there's a passing on of what people offer from generation to generation. But the church is also very inclusive because there's a team around the families ensuring we're not exclusive.

It's a fun place.

About seven years ago we began to pray that God would fill in the gaps in our congregation, *says Anne*. There were a few families setting out on family life.

God has answered that prayer and brought many families and, therefore, children into our congregation. As a result we have been able to be part of an organisation called Mothers of Pre-Schoolers (MOPS). This has helped us to reach out to mothers in the community who need help with parenting. *(See* www.mops.org *for more information.)*

The teenagers who are part of our congregation through the youth work are welcomed and encouraged to take part fully in church life. A number of them have been encouraged and financially supported through outreach and development courses run by DNA and Youth With a Mission (YWAM). As they become more mature they are brought on to young leadership programmes.

*DNA offers its trainees year-long placements described as 'church-based discipleship in the context of mission'. See* www.dna-uk.org. *YWAM has 1,200 ministry centres located all over the world. (See* www.ywam.org.)

During the summer we organise a trip for all ages. The young people say they enjoy being part of the group with older people. Usually activities are planned such that everyone can participate, from visiting sites of interest, visiting a play park and, more importantly, all having afternoon tea together.

The concern is that we lose some of the group as adults but our hope is that the input instilled in their lives will have an impact later and give them something to cling on to should they meet problems along life's way.

\* \* \*

There's a wonderful quote attributed to Henry Ford *(American founder of the Ford Motor Company)*: 'If you always do what you've always done, you'll always get what you've always got.' But we've always done what we did in the 1970s, when there were hundreds of young people. The Church has stayed the same; society hasn't. Back in the 1960s and 1970s, if you wanted something to do in the evening, there was the Boys' Brigade, the Girl Guides, church youth groups and so on. And you went to whatever was on in your local church. But young people have moved on. The idea of wearing a uniform doesn't appeal. Young people wear a school uniform all day and want to get out of it. And specialise ... martial arts, hockey, riding, clubs, whatever. You see the hope in them and it's doing these activities that helps them flourish. The BB *has* changed and evolved (and I'm a BB officer), but we have to think about how we engage with young people.

For example, at our church we have several people who are or used to be teachers. We've got prelim exams coming up at the school. We could offer space in our church for revision. Open up the Wi-Fi and invite young people along. And we have the people to call upon to offer them a bit of tuition. We've got to offer something more than just a Sunday service for the young folk. Do something like this and you plant a seed – they remember that 'the church helped me'. Actions speak louder than words.

\* \* \*

*Bankfoot's new church centre in Perthshire has been designed so that partnerships with other local organisations can thrive and young people and families engage with a range of activities.*

We host Bankfoot School's Out, an after-school club. It's privately run but it's non-profit, and everyone involved is trained of course. And there's a mother and toddlers group here on a Wednesday.

Then we've hired a part-time youth worker and we run two youth groups. There's Compass, which is for younger children, and The Hub for the older ones. They both run three days a week.

Dance and drama groups used to meet in the village hall but now they meet here.

And as more young people and their families come through the church-centre doors, more relationships are made and more activities planned. We have plenty of car parking and we now host conferences, fiftieth-anniversary meals and so on. (And we've a catering group that could feed the five thousand.)

\* \* \*

Actually, I think we can be a bit obsessed about young people. I'm not really sure there ever were young people, at least not in the way we think about it. They were there, in church, but not necessarily of their own volition.

We have roughly sixty members in our kirk session, with an average age that is over, say, 55. We've got just two young people who are 19 or 20 – but they're not ordained elders, they are 'associated' with the session.

In our session a lot elders sign off at 70 and become elders *emeriti*. I think it's a shame people feel they have to do that because sometimes older people have quite a lot of wisdom and experience to offer.

\* \* \*

*It's a big problem in rural areas. Ian Maclagan worships in the rural parish of Bute and knows the whole Presbytery of Argyll well.*

Youngsters go off to university and never come back. There's a vast gap between children left at school and people who are near retiring. The Presbytery of Argyll planned to employ three youth education ministries but our quota of employees was cut back so we went down from three to two: two youth education ministries working with congregations and young people throughout the length and breadth of the presbytery. They are bringing the ministry of the Word and encouraging young people to attend church. And the purpose of these ministries is not necessarily to provide hands-on youth work but to be facilitators and advisers to churches on how to invite young people back into the fold. But because the coverage provided by the ministries (one is a minister and one is not) is over the whole Presbytery of Argyll, it's very fragmented.

\* \* \*

Between Tarbert and Campbeltown (a distance of thirty-seven miles), but excluding Campbeltown itself, there are eleven children in Church of Scotland Sunday Schools.

That's over three congregations, including in Tarbert, which has a population of around 1,200 people.

\* \* \*

We have an awful lot of children around us and we run a Sunday club every week. Three families come most Sundays but there are a lot more out there. We are a growing congregation – we're bucking the trend – but some folk have stopped coming. And there's something about the ruralness of the community that means whole families come – not just one child. So if you lose them, you're losing a whole family.

We hope to introduce Messy Church but we're only a small church and that would be a big commitment.

\* \* \*

We have a youth club on Friday night, run by the same man who runs the Sunday School – there's that input for teenagers. And we've run Messy Church three times a year – that's been quite successful. We should make more of an effort, perhaps, but Messy Church is quite an effort in itself. It was a joint venture run for the three churches between Tarbert and Campbeltown, and we included Gigha too, so we had to time it with the ferry. (In the Highlands and Islands, the Church of Scotland works to the rules of the Church of Scotland *and* Calmac ferries.) So it's an effort – but forty or fifty years ago people gave up every Friday night to run the Boys' Brigade and so on.

\* \* \*

My own relationship with younger people in the church is a very good one because I've been involved with them in several ways – mainly by taking part in things they organise. We support an organisation in Malawi and the youngsters go out every second year, and they raise funds for the trips. They've arranged meals, *Ready, Steady, Cook* evenings and a murder mystery that included a three-course meal. And we support all these things. Not because I'm an elder but because I want to be there – though *because* I'm an elder, people note that I am there.

I was once called 'cool' by a young person. And that was a compliment, I think!

\* \* \*

My experience was that it was precisely the elders who did keep me in church because, at certain points when I was a teenager, it wasn't going to be my parents.

One elder, who was also a Sunday School leader, kept me going. A relationship of trust meant something to me. One time, she asked me to help her set up the Christmas decorations in church. This was my first sense of recognition and it was specifically because I was asked to help – I could be of service. And we chatted together. We were speaking adult to adult, not adult to child. It's probably something that elders are in a better position to do. Interaction with ministers is because they are ministers. Elders are ordinary people.

I'm not sure it's true that organisations keep young people in church. It's relationships – and often relationships across the generations. The 70-plus generation would have people round – they knew the person down the street. And they know how to build relationships in a way that I'm not sure younger people do – at least not in the same way.

# 9

# 'To See Oursels as Others See Us'

*Although Robert Burns once advocated the discipline (in his poem 'To a Louse'), nevertheless it may not be an especially Presbyterian occupation to reflect on how other people see us. It smacks of immodesty. And yet if part of the point of being an elder is to help make a difference in one's church and community, then the question seems valid – however diffidently we answer it. How do others see you? The flip side of that question is another one: In what ways has your life changed since becoming an elder? They are questions that can reveal surprising insights and glimpses of profound vulnerability.*

How do I perceive myself as an elder? No differently from everyone else in the church. In my role as an elder, am I the type of person who others within the church would come to with problems, for help or for prayer perhaps? I find that a difficult question to answer. Looking back, maybe yes; however, these have not been frequent occurrences.

\* \* \*

I am seen as an example – for good or ill.

\* \* \*

*As a younger man soon to start training to become a Church of Scotland minister (and so, in the traditional terminology, a 'teaching elder'), Andrew Rooney doesn't believe he is alone in growing up with a rather limited view of what an elder is.*

Most people think of elders as doing the business of the church. They support the minister, they serve communion dressed in black and they visit people and drink tea with them. As some newer elders come on board, the wearing of black is not so prevalent. But my mum was an elder and when she began, everyone wore black because that was the thing to do. Black *was* the thing for communion. Suits for men, skirts and tops or suits for women; certainly really smart clothes. There was not a great deal of colour around communion.

\* \* \*

I'm regarded as a happy person. They don't defer to me in any way because I'm an elder, and I prefer it that way. Two years ago we had a talent night. Another elder and myself did a comic routine, which shows that the elders are not necessarily fuddy duddy! There were a lot of youngsters at that too, and it was good they saw us like this. We like our fun!

\* \* \*

In the community I get 'and you, an elder of the kirk …!' when I say something people don't expect. People don't swear or are careful with what they say around me, or at least they can be.

There was a day when being an elder was something that people aspired to be. A banker arriving in a new job and getting himself invited to be an elder – that would get him a tick by his name at head office as being a good thing. But it wouldn't count for anything nowadays.

In church a lot of us are involved in prayers, on door duty, counting the money – that sort of thing. I suspect a lot of people think that's what an elder is about – policing the place and making sure the money is counted properly (a *very* serious business, that!).

\* \* \*

I have been an elder for a long time and so the change it has made to my life has been rather blurred. I suppose it gave me a better understanding – sometimes frustratingly – of the workings of the church locally. Having lived through the tenure of four different ministers since becoming an elder, it has been interesting to see their different approaches.

I have no idea how others see me!

I had a reputation for speaking out when I didn't agree and was once congratulated at a church AGM for managing to close the ministry and leadership committee I had been chairing because other committees were duplicating our work.

I get on with most people but find those who take themselves too seriously tedious.

I now probably take less of a front seat because I have been on so many committees over the years. I felt it was time for younger people to become more involved, including my daughter, who became an elder about four years ago.

\* \* \*

*Douglas Robertson speaks as an elder of only three years' standing, having been ordained at the age of 26. Already very involved in the life of his congregation, he is also an officer in the Boys' Brigade.*

Becoming an elder made a difference at BB. Previously, if any of the boys guessed my age they'd get it more or less right. But now, when they hear I'm an elder in the church, all of a sudden I'm in my mid-thirties or forties! It's the term elder – it means older to them, which is interesting. I know their perception of age is at a certain level – even at 28 I'm 'over the hill', but that's their perception of elders.

Within a session I'm still seen as 'the boy', which I think is not going to change until I move on elsewhere. I've grown up with them and they don't want to think of me as old, because that means they're getting old too.

There are times when I get on to a bit of rant. I came back from a conference with other young elders (*organised by the Church of Scotland's Mission and Discipleship Council in September 2013*) and reported back to the session. And I could tell that one or two thought, 'He's back on his soapbox again.' And it comes back to a perception of youthful inexperience.

I think churches are good at pigeonholing you. If you're young you work with the young people – that's all you do.

* * *

*Pat Johnston has worked as a senior social worker for South Ayrshire Council and also managed a retirement home in Ayr.*

Perhaps I should say that my life now revolves around the church, since in the past I only attended on a Sunday and had no further involvement. As a presbytery elder I had the opportunity to visit Malawi in 2010 – to say the least, it was a life-changing experience and one I shall always cherish. Also that same year, with the Presbytery of Ayr, I visited Oberammergau to see the Passion Play. Both experiences have had a lasting effect and I no longer take things such as food for granted. I would also hope that my previous experiences during my career have equipped me to recognise need and with the knowledge and desire to effect change for the better.

I hope others see me as a person who can be trusted, has empathy and a working knowledge and commitment to 'the greater need' of others.

I would not say that I have a strong faith, but I do feel a sense of well-being within myself. I am also aware that I need to have a 'purpose' for my life, and perhaps being involved in the work of the church – particularly in addressing the needs of the community – is also meeting my own need, as well as others'.

* * *

*Hugh Paterson's experience of the eldership has been in the rural linked charge of Gigha and Cara with Kilcalmonell with Killean and Kilchenzie. He has found that, in the local communities, the kirk session and elders still have a prominent role that is not always so immediately evident in urban settings.*

The session does have a broad community role. Everybody knows everybody else. There was a danger of the local shop closing down. The church got involved in saving it. We bought the folk out and, because we weren't shopkeepers ourselves, we sold it on to people who were. There's an issue with rural schools closing too. I have some sympathy with councils that are trying to keep all these schools open but we were involved in saving our school. And yes, sure, it was something the elders could take a lead in. The elders are the same people who are on the village-hall committee and managing the wind-farm funds. *(Local communities receive income from the companies that build wind turbine 'farms' and committees are set up to distribute the money to local projects.)*

In the rural areas the elder is often seen as a leader in the community. Not in Tarbert, which is quite a large village and people do not go to church. But I can remember the days, fifty or sixty years ago, if you required a job reference you'd get one from the minister and the session clerk. That wouldn't happen now. But back then it would have been the case that the bank manager, the doctor, the magistrate – they would all have been elders. The elder-ship has widened now – it's less 'professional'; it isn't just the worthies on it. But they are still leaders in the community.

\* \* \*

I was a missionary in Africa. I was teaching at Chogoria Girls Primary School for six years. I had to go for an inter-view with the committee of the missionary society. All the members were men. Being an elder certainly helped me.

In Chogoria I was known as an elder and treated as such. Within the Presbyterian Church of East Africa, being an elder is regarded as a great honour. I served communion at the evening services – which were mainly for hospital people and white folk. I was never asked to serve communion at the morning service though.

\* \* \*

Hopefully I am seen as a caring and approachable servant of the Church

\* \* \*

Others have told me that I work very hard for the church, have a good knowledge of the Bible and am a good elder. I think I'm seen to be loyal to the minister and congre-gation, and have a good knowledge of how the Church of Scotland works. What they say behind my back is another matter!

Over the years I think I have come to realise the importance of teamwork. Everyone has a share in Christ's ministry and it's not just about a few stars and the employed minister.

* * *

Within church I'm well respected because of the amount of work that I do in the place or organise. Yes, I'm very well respected. I'm also quite a jovial person and that helps.

Within the community there are several people who say, 'The work you and your wife get involved in in the village is tremendous.' I restarted the Boys' Brigade here in Bankfoot and I was president and then secretary of the bowling green.

*Though Alec Melville has been an elder for over twenty years there was a time – when his life seemed at its most fragile – when he felt he could not undertake the duties.*

There was a period when everything went wrong. Partly it was because of my job. We moved to Dunfermline and I still went to church every Sunday. I was just working all the time. The minister asked me to be an elder but I said, 'No, sorry.'

Then the story all goes sour. My wife and I split up. There was no way I was going to be an elder.

Alice (my second wife) and I got involved. There was a period when I was not going to church every Sunday. Alice and I were living together but we were not married, so we didn't go to church. But there was a missing link for us, gnawing signs that this was not right. We knew what it was.

The first time I went to the Laigh Kirk (in Paisley), it was a Christmas Eve service. I felt quite embarrassed. I felt I couldn't be an elder. I wasn't going to embarrass the church in that way. No way. But I did start going back to church, in Paisley, and eventually this is where I started serving as an elder again.

* * *

I have been divorced, remarried and become the father of three adopted children. I have been involved in active leadership, then was not involved at all and uncertain of just about every doctrine, but now have renewed confidence in the love of God in Christ.

I think other people in my congregation would see me as someone who is flawed yet confident about being loved by God. I am also aware that I have served as an elder in four congregations, each of which was very different (two in priority areas, one city and one new town). To some degree each context probably shaped how I was viewed. For example, I was considered very wealthy in Ferguslie Park because I had a car and had bought a house! I am also aware that my life story – particularly in relation to my divorce – means that some people in other congregations to which I used to belong may consider me someone selfish and reckless.

One young person with whom I worked for a good number of years in Ferguslie Park later came to visit me when I worked for the YMCA. He had known me as his youth worker and an elder in the church, which happened to be less than 100 yards from his house in the scheme.

He had been in my home many times and he had also grown fond of my ex-wife. We had been on camps together, been abroad and he had attended my father's funeral. For years I had tried to encourage him to believe that God was for him.

On the day in question he looked at me and told me that he had recently realised that God could just possibly be for someone like him. I thought of something I might have said or done over the years that might have helped him to that conclusion. It was profoundly shocking to me when he went on to say, 'It was when you got divorced.'

He went on to say that my best endeavours and my Christian world view had led him to believe I was essentially better than, or different from him. This was a belief likely founded on a perception of my position as one of authority and moral virtue as well as on my relative material wealth. And so he believed that God was really for people like me and not him. My divorce shattered many of his illusions, not least because I had been the one who left. If God could still be for me then, he concluded, maybe God could be for him too.

# Decision makers

*Elders are often required to be decision makers at all levels of the Church's structures. They speak here about their experiences of being members of local kirk sessions, presbytery elders, commissioners to the General Assembly, and as members of national councils or committees.*

## At kirk session

Decision making within St Quivox Church in Ayr is normally taken in the kirk session and congregational board meetings and is subject to a vote from members in attendance. There are occasions when the vote is not necessarily in accordance with one's own view, but one must accept gracefully the decision of the majority – and perhaps decide to postpone the matter, for further discussion, until a later date!

\* \* \*

*Isobel Alford's experience is of a kirk session of just six members representing a small, rural congregation.*

Our kirk session meets fairly regularly. The meetings last an hour and a half, rarely more. We've an agenda and we have a minute taker. But we're free to say what we want to say. Undoubtedly there is a family atmosphere – it's a very strong feature of the church. We regard ourselves as a family. I haven't been present at a session meeting where there's any real argument. When there are differences of opinion we're very careful about how we deal with each other. Which is nice – but not always effective. Maybe it means you don't always move on as you should. But this doesn't happen very often; we agree on the big things.

As a kirk session we are very supportive of the minister. He has told us he has appreciated, and placed huge importance on, the knowledge that we are supporting him through very difficult times in prayer. This has grown my own faith because I realise there is not only a place in the eldership for supporting the congregation but also for supporting the minister. We are honest with him as well. If there's stuff that he's doing or not doing, we will take it to him.

\* \* \*

Coming out of the Baptist Church, where I was one of twelve deacons, I found it very difficult going into a kirk session with about forty to fifty elders in it. In the Baptist Church, from a faith commitment point of view there was a different attitude to meetings. People's thinking was more faith-orientated.

Having said that, the people here are lovely – excellent to be alongside. But I'm not sure our thinking is always set in that obvious faith context. I'd be quite careful what I said. In a large group you may say something that someone else might have difficulty accepting, and the group is too large to work it out. At one time I'd have gone headlong into an issue in top gear. But not everyone necessarily feels the same way you do about different issues in the Church, so sometimes it's better to keep quiet. You don't want to offend – whereas when there were just twelve deacons, it was a small enough group to work things out when we disagreed with each other.

\* \* \*

Elders can do so much in the church. They can do the background jobs that have to happen. Where the model falls down, *argues Andrew Rooney*, is when you walk into a church and there's a congregation of a hundred, and forty or fifty of them are elders. That's too many for the session meeting because everyone will have an opinion on something. And that's difficult. I'd have thirty and no more. The smaller the number the easier it is to get them on the bus and get the bus moving.

I was working in a Glasgow city church that had a management team with six or seven people on it. They made most of the decisions that went back to the eldership – and if they agreed, they went ahead.

*On discovering that another minister had adopted a similar model, Andrew asked him how his elders had felt about not making all the decisions.* The minister told them,

'The main job of the elder is to be an example to the rest of the flock. I want you to be a witness in the community we live in.' They were still going to have the space to talk, to think, to strategise. But he used the management team to make the bigger decisions. And I think that's the way forward. When I was at school, if you had a group of fifteen, you couldn't get to an agreement – there were strong opinions and someone would be offended. But if you had five, say, that would work. Giving people a voice within a smaller leadership team increases the amount of change that can be made.

\* \* \*

We have about fifty elders, including several elderly ones who are not really participating. You can't ask them to resign – it would cause an awful upset. But they are not able to get out and about. So we have added elders.

If an elder doesn't do anything, there's nothing you can do about it. There's no authority. I always thought that being the session clerk was like being a sergeant in the army. I tried to keep the other ranks in order and stop the minister from doing anything daft.

\* \* \*

Within our own church one thing that disturbs me a little bit is the age-range of the eldership. We don't seem to be getting any younger elders. I'll be 85 soon; I think I'd like to make room for younger people. We've got quite a few younger people who are taking an active part in church life. There are many in their thirties to fifties who would be very good elders. Some are put off, I think, because there's a fear that if things go pear-shaped they may have to sell their houses. *(This concern relates to the role of elder as a charity trustee for the local congregation – see footnote on elders and liabilities in* Eldership in the Church of Scotland, *p. xiii.)*

\* \* \*

*St Andrew's Parish Church, Arbroath, is one congregation that has taken a hard look at how it organises its decision making. The role of elders within the kirk session has been rethought to make decisions more effectively and enable those not elders to become more involved in the vision and growth of the congregation. Together, Audrey Brown and Doug Hamilton describe a little of the impact of these changes.*

Audrey: Have there been changes in what is expected of an elder? Yes, mainly because of the change in the constitution.

Doug: The decision-making role of the elder has markedly changed. The forming of a leadership group has been very successful.

Audrey: We have a leadership team, consisting of twelve members and comprising both elders and non-elders. Then there are core groups covering fabric, finance, worship, nurture and so on, with a person in charge and a small group of about eight. And there's a link person from the leadership team. Then there's the session, which has ultimate trusteeship of the congregation. They say yea or nay to whatever the leadership group of one of the core groups proposes.

The session used to meet more often. It's quarterly now; it would have been monthly. Before, we would have had the opportunity to get into small groups for discussion and debate about any issues coming up. I miss that, where you get everyone together and you get the nuances of what people are feeling.

Doug: It has proved that the smaller group is able to discuss, manage business more precisely and quicker than with a kirk session comprising thirty to forty elders.

Audrey: It's different. It feels more like an organisation. But we've grown in numbers and a larger congregation has different needs.

Doug: The kirk session now meets to confirm and approve decisions made by the leadership team. So I'd say my role as an elder of St Andrew's has changed quite considerably.

## In presbytery

*Pat Johnston was a member of the Presbytery of Ayr for six years.*

Contrary to my expectations, I did not find presbytery a very 'welcoming' experience for a lay person. I only spoke once during my term of office. I understand there is now a booklet, explaining the terms and procedures used and church law, but at that time I felt superfluous. Also, I wondered how ministers found time to complete the duties required by their own church, having undertaken additional duties at presbytery. I was also aware that some ministers must have put considerable preparation into their responses.

\* \* \*

I was a member of the Presbytery of Edinburgh for a brief period. Its procedures have changed since that time but I do have an abiding memory of the atmosphere perforated by the whistling of hearing aids that were being adjusted to allow their wearers to participate; it seemed to encapsulate the difficulties of the church in more ways than one. However, that was in the twentieth century!

\* \* \*

*Andrew Kimmitt was 22 when he was ordained an elder at Morningside United Church in Edinburgh.*

Last year I was asked to be a presbytery elder, which was odd for one so young. A presbytery elder is often the senior or *a* senior member of their kirk session. In the Presbytery of Edinburgh there were perhaps three or four of us under the age of 40, including one or two training for the ministry. At 22 I was easily the youngest there. And the presbytery clerk reckoned that I was the youngest they'd ever had in the presbytery.

In theory I could have – should have – been involved in one of the presbytery committees, but I don't have time for that. (I'm also a member of the Council of Assembly; it takes up a lot of time.) *(The Council is a national body appointed by the General Assembly to take administrative decisions between annual assemblies.)*

Edinburgh has a huge presbytery – about 130 voting members. In a typical meeting with typical debates, it is unlikely that I am going to stand up and say anything. That's not just because I'm young; it's a general thing. If they are making a decision about spending £6,000 for repairs, not many people are going to speak. And a lot of the time, all the business is decided beforehand. The presbytery is sort of rubber-stamping.

\* \* \*

Presbytery elders should change every two years to give fresh perspectives.

\* \* \*

I was a presbytery elder followed by being a 'freely elected' elder for a total of eight years about twenty years ago. I was also a commissioner to the General Assembly twice about twenty and fifteen years ago.

My experience as presbytery elder – I was on the social and community interests committee and, through that, Edinburgh Churches Together – was useful, not only in getting to know the workings of the Church better but, as this was also during my time on the committee of L'Arche, Edinburgh, my role as elder enabled me to make contacts with other denominations. This benefited L'Arche at the time as the Edinburgh community was in its infancy.

*(L'Arche is an international faith community, founded by Jean Vanier in France in 1964, where people with and without learning disabilities share their lives together. For more information go to* www.larche-edinburgh.org.uk*.)*

I must confess meetings of presbytery could be rather turgid, but not always. The greatest benefit of these experiences was when we had a vacancy at short notice before the summer holidays. As joint session clerk (my other half was going on holiday) I was left to arrange a locum and so on. We were not given an interim moderator until after the holidays. It was not easy but at least I was familiar with presbytery proceedings and knew who the presbytery clerk was.

\* \* \*

*Maureen Mackinnon believes she has been able to make a real change through her position as a presbytery elder.*

I'm a member of the Presbytery of Argyll and I'm on the ministries committee. I've done that for three years and one of the things I was keen on was mentoring *(a scheme whereby a newly ordained minister is supported by one with longer experience).*

A minister came to another charge on our island and they'd just finished their probationary year. They didn't have a mentor and there began to be problems. They had a pastoral carer but a mentor is different. Ministers need the support of someone who's done it – who has experience (though whether they'll use them or listen to them is another thing). So I was keen on getting a mentoring scheme going. It's in its early stages but it's started.

\* \* \*

Eldership on an island is different from many other places, *suggests Hamish Taylor*, especially as an elder in presbytery. I was a member of the small Presbytery of Uist. We called ourselves a small presbytery and that might imply that we had little inkling of what was going on in the higher echelons of the Church. But because there were so few of us, every elder was in at the deep end of everything that goes on. In a tiny presbytery everybody – ministers and elders – are at the sharp end. In the Presbytery of Uist we didn't have any committees. We appointed individuals to do the different tasks. But each of these individuals was very accountable to presbytery as a whole – and most of these tasks were undertaken by elders.

When elders became eligible to become moderators of presbytery in 1996, I was elected as moderator in 1997 – I think I was the second elder-moderator in Scotland. And I was elected again in 2003. One elder-moderator of the Presbytery of Uist was elected for four consecutive years. I wonder if that's happened anywhere else in Scotland. It was because of his wisdom. At the time, our discussions with Edinburgh *(the administrative offices of the Church of Scotland)* over ministry allocations were rather fraught and this elder had the skill of seeing reality through all the fog.

## At the General Assembly

I'm not a very political person. I choose not to get involved in the politics and the General Assembly. But that may change – because as an elder in the church I need to be more informed.

\* \* \*

I think elders who are simply commissioned to the General Assembly for a single year and then never go back again have very little to contribute.

\* \* \*

I am not a member of presbytery but I have twice represented the congregation at the General Assembly.

The Assembly is interesting but, on first attendance, overwhelming. You have to be desperate about an issue and brave to speak up. It seems to run with those in the know and there are too many of the same faces doing all the talking. I don't think a lot of the views aired are really representative of the wider Church. It is, however, very educational about what is going on in the Church of Scotland, and you do learn a lot.

\* \* \*

I am not a member of presbytery but have on several occasions attended the General Assembly. I have been amazed and impressed by the depth and honesty of the debates, some of which, I must admit, I found stressful and difficult – and, to be honest, quite hard to understand.

\* \* \*

I have never been a presbytery elder. However, I have attended the General Assembly on three occasions. The first was in 1999 when I had the privilege of serving communion. This was an experience I will never forget, ensuring that the group served over 800 people with communion. This was the year the General Assembly was held in Edinburgh's Exhibition Centre because the new Scottish Parliament was using the Assembly Hall.

Each morning the worship is always like nothing ever experienced in the local setting, with the Assembly commissioners singing the hymns with such conviction. I find the worship also sets the tone each day for the discussion and deliverances from the different councils within the Church.

All three assemblies have been very different and I think this may be due to how the different moderators bring their own gifts in moderating the meeting and also because it is not the same ministers and elders who attend each year. From Glasgow, commissioners are appointed approximately every four years on a rota basis.

I have found it is an opportunity for individual councils to celebrate the work that they have done over the past year and set out the plan for the coming year or future years when reporting back.

I often find that when decisions come to a vote you have to decide what your personal feeling on a particular subject is. But most importantly you are there representing your congregation and must work out what a decision may mean to your congregation and community.

I think attending the General Assembly has given me a better awareness of the work of the wider Church, both at home and abroad.

\* \* \*

At the General Assembly, although I was aware of 'tradition', I thought the mechanism slow and some matters for discussion considerably out of date. Overall it was an experience I enjoyed. Sometimes I wish the 'voice' of the Church could be heard in matters concerning the welfare of our people; so often it is silent.

\* \* \*

*Among the most moving and memorable moments of any General Assembly are those occasions when a commissioner feels able to speak from personal experience or with direct knowledge about a particular situation or cause. Jamie Stuart was one of those.*

It has always been my desire to be a commissioner at the Assembly, and in 1992 and in 2013 the kirk session of High Carntyne Church in Glasgow invited me to have the honour of attending at the Mound in Edinburgh. That first time, in 1992, I took my seat near the front of the action and was thrilled to join with 1,000 voices singing the opening hymn.

Fast-forward twenty-one years and my church, once again, invited me as a commissioner to the Assembly. At my advanced age I knew many members of the Church of Scotland (including several former moderators), and I looked forward hugely to the important week of deliberations.

On Monday morning, 20 July, I took my seat in the

huge Assembly Hall … As I waited for the proceedings to commence, my mind floated back to the year 1948 and the Edinburgh International Festival. In that year Sir Tyrone Guthrie produced *A Satire of the Three Estates* and decided that the Church of Scotland Assembly Hall was the most appropriate venue in the city. The production ran for three weeks to sell-out audiences.

At that stage in my life I was a professional actor and was cast as Sandy Solace, an inebriated courtier. Sitting in my seat as a well-behaved elder of the kirk, I recalled Sandy Solace bursting through the entrance doors of the Hall and running down the aisle and – at the top of my voice – yelling, 'Wow! Wha saw ever sic a throng?'

I guess we all have a cause to support as we try to make the world a better place. For some years now I have supported the Edinburgh-based Scottish charity ASH (Action on Smoking and Health, Scotland). As a commissioner to the Assembly I was aware I would be allowed to speak if my theme were appropriate and could be slotted into the business of the day.

On the Thursday of the week, the Church and Society Council gave its report and questions were invited. I was a wee bit nervous but, even so, put up my hand for permission to speak. I got the nod from the moderator. I was in the front row and stood up to my full five feet, three inches! 'Moderator, I want to raise awareness about the exploitation of tobacco farmers in developing countries by the tobacco industry …' *(Still the professional performer, Jamie concluded his speech by quoting with theatrical vitality from James VI's and I's 1604 treatise,* A Counterblaste to Tobacco.*)* Well – I got a sitting ovation to be sure! The Very Revd Albert Bogle stood up and declared, 'You have just heard from an elder who is probably the oldest commissioner in the hall. That was a speech given with passion! We can use more of that!'

\* \* \*

*For ten years Ian Maclagan has been clerk to the Presbytery of Argyll. In that role he has attended the General Assembly on many occasions. He has felt able to bring his particular skills and training to bear on certain occasions.*

I suppose I'm lucky. I understand the workings of the Church of Scotland. I've been involved in it heavily for ten years. I have been able to contribute where I thought it advantageous to do so. On one occasion I realised that one of the departments of the Church had been inadvertently misapplying a law, probably for years. I realised that the consequence of this was that one congregation in Argyll looked like it would have to lose £4,000 – a large amount – and I realised that this misinterpretation had caused the sum to be calculated wrongly. So the law had to be rewritten. It was an instance where my legal training was useful. Not everyone is necessarily going to be a pastoral elder but we can all use our own particular skills.

\* \* \*

In theory, presbytery and the General Assembly gives voice to elders of the church in decision making. In practice, I think there are a number of issues with this assumption.

Votes are too often swayed by speakers who have previously agreed with each other what they are going to say, in order to promote their own agendas.

Emotional appeals can also lead to unsound decisions being taken.

Those who have the gift of thinking on their feet are unfairly advantaged in debates while those who like to think about things beforehand are left behind – particularly when things come up at the last minute at the Assembly or in presbytery or session.

Generally, elders attend the Assembly only once or twice and are therefore unused to the way things work – whereas some, such as presbytery clerks or former moderators, are seasoned operators and use that to promote their own agendas.

Ministers attend presbytery throughout their tenure and sometimes into retirement. Elders are often there for a relatively short time and do not find their voice in debate. (The Presbytery of Glasgow is a large one!)

The spiritual content of Assembly or presbytery can get lost in debate

## Councils and committees

I think there is benefit in elders being involved in the work of the councils and the presbytery committees if they can offer feedback into their local congregation as well as contribute to wider thinking and action in the Church.

* * *

*Andrew Kimmitt is an elder in his early twenties. He sits on the Council of Assembly, which has the authority to take administrative decisions between General Assemblies and coordinate the work of the Church's central administration. Members of the Council of Assembly are charity trustees for a large part of the Church of Scotland.*

It's quite intense. At my first meeting, I was there – a 22-year-old theology student in a room of lawyers, accountants, Reverend Doctors and past moderators. It has revealed a very, very different side of the Church. Any naivety you have about people just being nice to each other because it's the Church ... It's the kind of business you have in any institution of that size.

\* \* \*

*John Macgill has been closely involved with the work of two councils of the Church of Scotland. In both cases he feels that he was invited to be on committees more for his skills as a journalist than because he was an elder. His feelings about these experiences are mixed; nevertheless, he welcomed the opportunities to be an elder of the Church, painting on a broader canvas.*

When you live in a parish or community where there are already very accomplished 'missionaries' who reach into the community, who give pastoral care, and when you've got a highly accomplished minister, it's a relief to find there's something you can do – to find some effective way of using your talents. I've always been a strong believer in the idea that the more you are given, the more you think about how you share. It has been a gift to me that I've been able to represent the Church; to have a role on a national body.

*John's time as convener of the publishing committee was a difficult one and his personal views about what occurred remain strong.* My business suffered because I was spending an inordinate amount of time talking to people and trying to save jobs.

It all seemed so far away from my wider church experience. I didn't equate eldership in my own church with my role chairing what was in effect the board of a small publishing company. There was an invisible divider between that work and my own congregational friends and members on the session, where nothing had changed. A lot of members of session were only vaguely aware I was doing something at a national level. But that was OK. There was nothing superior about what I was doing – I was no better as an elder because I was serving at a national level. I was unusual in that I was a journalist/communicator using those skills for the wider Church.

I then rejoined the Social Care Council (which I had been on previously, helping guide the council towards its 'rebranding' as CrossReach), and it was so wonderfully free of personalities. It was an organisation that had a single, defined clear aim and purpose. It was selfless and struggling to do whatever it takes for those of every age who need support. There were inspirational leaders and staff there, dealing with front-end Christianity. It was hugely rewarding and I felt humbled to be put in a position of responsibility in an organisation with thousands of staff and thousands of people in their care.

*And John's advice to anyone invited to be on a council or committee?*

Before one accepts a role on any of these groups or committees, find out as much as you can about them. In one context I felt absolutely a fish out of water. Look carefully and see, in reality and however flattered you may be, if this is something that is really right for you.

# Appendix 1

# Resources

As elders have reflected on their experiences of, and feelings about, the role, they have also occasionally mentioned resources that have helped them over the years. They range from short prayers to General Assembly reports. They are listed here, together with other publications and website resources current at the time of writing.

## Mentioned in this book

Reports to the General Assembly of the Church of Scotland (accessed October 2013):

- 'A Church without Walls' (The Report of the Special Commission anent Review and Reform to the General Assembly of the Church of Scotland) 2001. Link available from the Church Without Walls page of the Church of Scotland website: www.churchofscotland. org.uk/connect/church_without_walls.
- 'The Report of the Special Commission anent Review and Reform to the General Assembly of the Church of Scotland 2003'.

Barclay, William, *The Gospel of Matthew (New Daily Study Bible)*, Volumes 1 and 2, Edinburgh: Saint Andrew Press, 2009.

Barclay, William, *The Letters of James and Peter (New Daily Study Bible)*, Edinburgh: Saint Andrew Press, 2011.

Barrett, C. K., *Church, Ministry and Sacraments in The New Testament*, Carlisle: Paternoster Press, 1985; reprinted 1993.

'The Eldership, Past and Present' (leaflet produced by the Church of Scotland Eldership Working Party): www.churchofscotland.org.uk/__data/assets/pdf_file/0007/3130/elder_rediscover.pdf.

Eldership Consultation: Background Papers and Consultation Summaries (ongoing at the time of writing). Links available from the Church of Scotland Resourcing Mission website: www.resourcingmission.org.uk/resources/eldership-consultation.

'Elders, liabilities and OSCR' (Circular of the Church of Scotland Law Department). Available on the Church of Scotland website (Links from Law Department Circulars): www.churchofscotland.org.uk/resources/subjects/law_circulars (revised October 2013).

## Personal suggestions by elders

Adam, David, books of prayers inspired by the traditions of Celtic spirituality, widely available.

Anon., 'Away in a Manger', last verse ('Be near me, Lord Jesus …'): 'a prayer to which I have regularly returned since my teenage years with different meaning in different contexts'.

de Mello, Anthony, a range of books on spirituality.

MacDonald, William Caldwell, *The Elder: Character and Duties*, Edinburgh: Saint Andrew Press, 1992.

Wiersbe, Warren W., *On Being A Servant Of God*, Michigan: Baker Books, revised edition, 2007.

Wild Goose Worship Resources: hymns, songs, prayers and resources from the Iona Community.

## And finally ...

'A simple prayer I often use is:

Dear Lord, help me to remember that nothing is going to happen today that you and I together won't be able to handle.'

# Appendix 2

# Questionnaire

The following questions made up the questionnaire that provided one way of gathering the experiences and stories of elders for this compilation. Rather than answer every question only briefly, elders were invited to choose three or four areas about which they felt they had something helpful or personal to contribute. A number responded to more. For this book we have tried, bearing in mind our desire for a range of chapters that reflect a diversity of opinion, to use as much of the material as possible. We have been able to use a high percentage of the responses in full or in part in the finalised chapters.

The questions are included here in the hope that they may provide the stimulus for discussion in groups, kirk sessions and local congregations – or that they will help elders and others to reflect personally about the role and the issues that the experiences of elders raise.

## 1 Becoming an elder

Describe any ways in which you experienced God's call as you made your decision to become an elder.

- What questions did you ask yourself and others before agreeing to become an elder?
- Were there particular conversations or events that helped you discern the way forward?
- What advice would you give to someone considering becoming an elder?


## 2 The Eldership Promise

Do you believe the fundamental doctrines of the Christian faith; do you promise to seek the unity and peace of the church; to uphold its doctrine, worship, government and discipline; and to take your due part in the administration of its affairs?

How do you apply the 'Eldership Promise'

a) to your encounters at church on a Sunday
b) in your day-to-day commitments and hopes for the church?

Can you share a story about when you have felt you were pursuing your call to the eldership most effectively?

## 3  Our spiritual lives

- In what ways has your faith grown or been challenged by being an elder?
- How do you find that your prayer life and/or reflection on scripture affects the ways you carry out your role?

## 4  Changes in the role

How do you feel about changes that have been introduced to the role and responsibilities of elders?

- Some changes might have been the requirement to be a trustee; the legislation around the safeguarding and protection of vulnerable groups.
- In what way do these changes match up with your original expectations of being an elder?

## 5  Hopes and dreams

How would you describe your congregation to a visitor or stranger now? What differences, if any, would you hope to see in your congregation in ten years' time?

- Can you identify particular opportunities?
- Do you have any aspirations for your congregation?

## 6 The pastoral role

- In what situation(s) have you offered pastoral support to others? What effect have these situations had on you?
- If you are able (*without giving names*) please give one or more specific examples in as much detail as you can, particularly focusing on the effect of the experience. *When we edit your stories, we will ensure that confidentiality is maintained.*

## 7 Elders and innovations (innovations you're involved with, including worship)

Can you describe ideas, projects or initiatives within your congregation – *especially within worship* – that you would describe as innovative?

- What is your role(s) in these?
- Would you like to pursue initiatives that are being frustrated?

## 8 Interacting with children and teenagers

- In what ways do you and your congregation interact with children and teenagers?
- Describe the joys and concerns of this area of your church life, with any examples you can provide.

## 9 How do people see you?

- In what ways has your life changed since becoming an elder?
- How do you think others see you – members of your own congregation; members of your community?

## 10 Making decisions

- Describe the ways you help make decisions within the Church.
- If you are a member of presbytery or have attended the General Assembly, we'd be very interested to hear your impressions of those experiences.